GARDEN FURNITURE
DESIGN & CONSTRUCTION

GARDEN FURNITURE
DESIGN & CONSTRUCTION

ANTONY JACKSON

DAVID & CHARLES
Newton Abbot   London   North Pomfret (Vt)

AUTHOR'S NOTE

The author is willing to help any reader with a significant design or construction problem relating to the projects and ideas put forward in this book. He is also happy to supply the items illustrated, or adaptations on a particular theme, either in assembled form or as a kit. He may be contacted by post c/o Waveney Cottage, Outney Road, Bungay, Suffolk. Please supply a stamped addressed envelope with your enquiry.

British Library Cataloguing in Publication Data

Jackson, Antony
    Garden furniture design and construction.
    1. Outdoor furniture—Amateurs' manuals
    I. Title
    684.1'8   TT197.5.09

    ISBN 0-7153-8944-0

Typeset by Typesetters (Birmingham) Ltd,
Smethwick, West Midlands
and printed in Great Britain
by Butler & Tanner Limited, Frome and London
for David & Charles Publishers plc
Brunel House   Newton Abbot   Devon

Published in the United States of America
by David & Charles Inc
North Pomfret   Vermont 05053   USA

Contents

Introduction   6
Suitability · Position and proportion · Texture · Colour

1   The English Garden   10
Weathervane · Covered seat · Arched bridge · Bench ·
Dovecotes · Stone seat · Curved seat · Trellised porch ·
Summerhouse · The opportunity for experiment · Formal
perspective

2   The New England Garden   26
Garden fence · Trellised porch · Square summerhouse ·
Octagonal summerhouse · Deck · Garden shed · Swinging seat
· Rustic pergola · Lakeside pavilion · Martin house · Gazebo ·
Garden chair · Rustic swinging chair · Twenty-first century
garden furniture

3   General Construction Principles   47
Multi-facet structures · Jig and template construction ·
Windows · Making tight dowelled mortice and tenon joints ·
Timber · Timber treatments · Tools

4   Projects   63
1 Arboured path · 2 Trellis · 3 Footbridge · 4 Wildfowl
nesting box · 5 Oak bench · 6 Picnic table · 7 Tree house/play
centre · 8 Cottage dovecote · 9 Wall-mounted dovecotes ·
10 Gate · 11 Revolving summerhouse · 12 Pergola ·
13 Corner house · 14 Simple bridge · 15 Garden and patio
whatnot · 16 Bird table

Index   159

Acknowledgements   160

Introduction

The aims of this book are twofold. Firstly to interest the reader in the design of garden furniture which is in sympathy with the overall garden plan rather than as an unrelated appendage that has just been 'stuck on'. Secondly to show how the normally practical person can produce very attractive and substantial pieces using simple construction and assembly techniques. Most of the projects are illustrated with photographs taken during significant stages of production, and with a colour photograph of the finished item.

Each project is offered in the knowledge that the construction techniques which are described do *work* and are appropriate. The evidence of this is in the photographic record. The professional woodworker may very well criticise some of the techniques used, saying 'I would not do it that way'. In a professional workshop environment he may be correct; indeed there are many things that I do differently in commercial manufacture. The main thrust of the book however is to suggest simple and practical answers to constructional problems for the ordinary person – the book is not offered as a professional reference text. The more knowledgeable or adventurous reader may well choose to adopt different techniques, or develop the scale and content of particular projects, using the book as a general guide. The degree of such development will usually depend on the time available and equipment at hand.

All the items described in the book conform to my personal view of what is good design. In broad terms design is a combination of suitability for the intended purpose, position and proportion, texture and colour. It is useful to consider each of these factors in turn.

Suitability

The trip to the local garden centre is usually undertaken with a very clear view of what is needed, whether it be a garden shed to put tools in, a seat for the garden or a fish pond. It is often provoked by the 'For heavens' sake I can't get into the garage anymore – there is so much rubbish' syndrome. This leads to a Saturday morning expedition to buy an 8×6ft (2.5×1.5m) larch lap shed. The mistake usually made is in not thinking the problem right through,

which would mean buying a shed that will not only store the lawnmower but also allow enough room for the workshop bench or a second freezer. Murphy's law states that an 8×6ft (2.5×1.5m) shed can only carry one lawnmower, two garden chairs, fifty-six tins of paint and a roll of old carpet (we may need it one day). Murphy's law goes on to say that when you need to get the lawnmower out you will first have to move two garden chairs, a roll of old carpet and fifty-six tins of paint, one of which will get squashed under the lawnmower wheels.

The key to suitability is usually size. It is reasonable to expect that, if you buy a fish pond, it will be suitable for its primary purpose. The *degree* of suitability for any design's particular purpose will normally be dictated by its size, perhaps combined with a design feature that allows better use to be made of the space available. An example of this would be the provision of a door at either end of the garden shed, giving a better than even chance of flouting Murphy's law. Unfortunately, Murphy's second law states that however large your garden shed is it will never actually be large enough! As yet there is no known way around this particular problem.

Position and Proportion

One of the consistently mystifying things about many gardens is the contrast between the gardener's specific appreciation of colour and design in individual flower beds and his seeming inability to treat the overall garden scheme with the same care, Murphys third law (otherwise known as Brussels Sprouts Syndrome) states that in every town or village in England there will be a beautiful lawned garden bordered by a vegetable patch full of monstrously ugly Brussels sprouts. The problem is not that there is anything wrong with Brussels sprouts but rather that their enormous, ugly open structure is often not in keeping with the surroundings. I have often noticed, when watching gardening programmes on the television, that the participants talk in glowing terms about how certain plants go together, perhaps with low shrubs providing contrast and scale for taller plants in the background. Then when the camera pans away to view the whole garden, this very interesting detail is lost in a flat, almost two-dimensional, overall picture. Thus, what is in its individual content a very interesting and colourful garden, blurs into a flat picture without scale or proportion in the broad overview. In my opinion this is caused by a failure to treat the whole garden with the same planning care given to individual beds.

The same rules apply to garden furniture and architecture. Every item should be scaled, designed and positioned in the garden so that it will *add* to the overall picture. To succeed in achieving proportion in the garden you may have to come to grips with Murphy's fourth law, which states that the most convenient place for a garden shed will always be in the worst possible position for garden design. This is backed up by the fifth law, stating that all long, narrow gardens will have a garden shed blocking most of the view.

Whenever possible the proportion of an article should reflect the proportion of the garden. In my view there are two main types of garden with varying degrees in between. These are *tall* gardens with good stands of mature indigenous trees, and *flat* gardens with no tall trees and very little growth over 10–12 feet (3–4m). The role of garden furniture should be to *add* to the established

character of a garden, and in a 'tall' garden this is best achieved with the use of 'tall' garden furniture, which serves to draw the eye upwards. Pergolas can be high, generously proportioned structures and summerhouse roofs may be steeply pitched, in sympathy with the shape of trees. In a 'flat' garden tall structures may only have a role towards the end of the property, creating a focal point that will help to foreshorten the view, and only then if there is a sufficient standard of foliage behind the structure. The danger of having any substantial structures in a 'flat' garden is that they will become more important than the plants they should be complimenting, particularly during the bare winter months. Care should be taken to keep visually obtrusive items to the edges of the property and to soften the hard lines of permanent structures with early and late flowering clematis or with evergreens such as cotoneaster and ivy.

While the role of garden furniture should be to complement the natural surroundings it is also important that the design of a particular item is satisfying in its own right. All too often the commercially available chalets and summerhouses are either grossly obtrusive in style, or mean in their proportions. I have time and again seen enormous, square summerhouses more suitable as beach huts, despoiling otherwise very attractive lawns. Their broad, squat shapes owe nothing to any thought of aesthetic design, but rather to cheapness of manufacture. Similarly there is a growing abundance of tiny octagonal, or hexagonal, wood and glass plant houses or summerhouses which, although perhaps functionally effective, can never look as though they are 'meant to be there'. Individual taste varies widely, and what matters at the end of the day is whether the owner likes what he or she has got.

Texture

The 'texture' of garden furniture comprises, for me, the type of material and the form in which it is used, and the main concern should be that the texture of an article is in keeping with the garden plan. A simple illustration of how unsuitable it can be is in the alloy climbing frames now so popular – their harsh angular texture can utterly destroy the soft lines and shapes of a garden. Similarly, I have seen sheds and other substantial structures clad with treated chipboard (composite boards), which presents a bland, uninteresting and thoroughly destructive aspect when compared with the interesting pattern of shiplap or tongue and groove timber used for the same purpose.

One of the most obvious textural problems is in the use of mineral felt on 'decorative' structures. This material adds nothing to a structure (in a design sense) and a tiled or

---

Below are what I hope will be some useful guidelines for the positioning of most irems so that they are in proportion to their environment.

Utilitarian Items Things (such as garden sheds) that you have to have, but in an ideal world would gladly be without.
- Always ensure that the structure is out of the direct line of vision whenever possible, even if this means putting it in a relatively inconvenient position.
- Always ensure that you cannot see any roof lines against the sky from the usual viewpoints. The structure should always be backed with high vegetation, helping to reduce its visual importance and scale.
- Always conceal at least part of the structure with climbing plants or ornamental trees. Use it as extra growing space.
- Consider whether the structure can be positioned to create a screen for the compost heap or vegetable patch.

Decorative Items Structures intended to be focal points in the garden.
- The further away (from the normal viewing position) a structure is, the larger it should be. There is no point in putting a two-foot (.6m) figurine 100 yards (91m) from the main viewpoint as visually it will be 'lost' to the garden design. The role of most decorative items, such as pergolas and dovecotes, should be to create a meaningful, and obviously intentional, point of interest. In long views these structures should also serve to provide scale for the plants and trees around them.
- The nearer an item is, the smaller it should be. The danger of having a summerhouse or similarly large structure close to the main viewpoint is that it will overpower the rest of the garden. Roof lines may be evident against the sky and the negative design impact may well overpower the positive functional aspect.

wooden roof should always be preferred. It is the difference between wearing a plastic mac or a couture raincoat from Aquascutum. Yet another textural problem is in the use of rustic poles to create formal garden structures. In my opinion this represents a textural imbalance – a formal pergola or screen should be designed and manufactured in materials that will give it an independent entity, so that the structure can shout out 'I am a pergola and I am meant to be here! look how attractive I am!'. With one or two exceptions, whenever I have seen a rustic pergola all it has said to me is 'I am a motley collection of old branches bashed together with 4in nails'. I think what really annoys me about rustic pergolas is that they are often built for the right reasons, but in the wrong form.

Colour

Even the most carefully designed and positioned structure can be completely destroyed by the application of a particular colour. In my view, at least in the English garden, the worst offender is the 'red wood' stain, so lovingly applied to anything that does not move. This lurid red colour does not match or respond to any indigenous species of tree, nor does it blend with the green grass. Use of red-wood colours in Scandinavian countries, or other areas forested with red woods is quite a different matter, but its role in the English country garden should be restricted. When choosing a colour for a structure always aim to reflect an existing natural colour, perhaps the pale shades of ash trees or the dark of some oaks. A colour that I find particularly useful in the English garden is 'walnut'.

In terms of proportional design you may like to consider some of the following ideas, and how they relate to your own needs.

Covered structures (sheds, summerhouses etc)
- Does the roof look as though it has been 'designed', or is it simply keeping the rain off? Consider roof pitch (too shallow?), degree of overhang (too little?).
- Will the structure blend into your garden environment? Will your carefully shaped beds and lawns clash with the square box of your intended structure, or would they respond better to the kinder lines of an octagonal or hexagonal shape?
- Are the window and door proportions sympathetic to the structure and to your own property? Large picture windows in a chalet are not necessarily going to blend ideally with the leaded lights of a period home.

Decorative Items
- Are the supporting posts for pergolas or screens in proportion with the structures they carry? 6in (15cm) posts supporting lengths of 2×2in (5×5cm) timber to make a pergola will look out of proportion.
- Is the structure large enough for the intended role? It is very easy to overestimate the size of things seen in a shop or garden centre which is packed with other products.

1 The English Garden

When I conceived the idea for a book on garden furniture, my thinking was primarily about the construction of wooden structures which broadly conformed to the accepted definition of garden furniture. The main text is certainly specifically concerned with this theme, from benches to summerhouses, but in researching for the book it soon became obvious that many other things should be considered as falling within its scope. Take, for example, the garden gate. Very often it is regarded simply as a necessary barrier, establishing territorial rights and keeping animals and children in – or out. Gates are normally fairly boring utilitarian affairs in wrought iron or wood, owing nothing to any sense of design and adding nothing to the character of house or garden. Now and again, however, one sees a gate that has been designed not just as a barrier but as a piece of garden architecture that sets the tone of house and garden. It almost goes without saying that anybody who has gone to the trouble and expense of designing and building such a gate will have devoted the same care and attention, in design terms, to the rest of the property. The gate, therefore, becomes an important piece of garden furniture.

This chapter, through its illustrations, takes a general look at the range of architecture, ornament and furniture that helps to give the 'English country garden' its deserved reputation throughout the world. Anybody asked to describe the English garden will certainly talk in terms of green lawns, summer flowers and roses. This is, of course, absolutely correct but in my view, not the whole truth. If asked to picture *my* English garden I would think of the terrace at Polesden Lacey in Surrey, the steep valley at Cragside in Northumberland or even my own in the Waveney valley in Suffolk. My picture of these gardens, and others too numerous to mention, would always include a piece of architecture or furniture. At Polesden Lacey my thoughts would be of a simple curved stone seat, set into a beautiful hedge along the terrace. At Cragside it would be the iron bridge spanning the valley near the house, and in my own garden it would be the revolving summerhouse set beneath tall ash trees. It is my submission that the really memorable English gardens all depend to a significant extent on their man-made elements.

The role of garden furniture in establishing the English garden character was best illustrated to me during a trip to the United States in which I visited the Vanderbilt mansion and the home of Franklin Roosevelt. Both houses are set in beautifully lawned and wooded grounds but neither has a single piece of architectural ornamentation or furniture away from the house – not even the rose garden, in which lies Roosevelt's grave and memorial. It is simply an area screened by a neat hedge with rows of rose bushes. Trees and lawns are as much the 'American garden' as flowers are the English garden, and the character of the grounds of both these important houses is entirely within context. It is difficult, however, to imagine a comparable English stately home without a complement of pergolas, walled gardens, statues, seats, summerhouses and temples. This, for me, sums up the charm and character of the English garden and as much as roses or croquet lawn makes it unique.

As a regular viewer of gardening programmes I am consistently disappointed in how little consideration seems to be given to the role of garden furniture and architecture as an important part of the overall garden plan. I think this happens because the main thrust of gardening is seen, by the presenters, to be *growing* – which is, after all, their trade. For me the English garden is more about *design*, and a critical and useful part of that design is garden furniture and architecture.

Perversely, the hurricane force winds that swept the southern and eastern counties of England during 1987 have emphasised the need for overall garden planning, ie including man-made structures. Many gardens have lost their tall trees and it will be years before new stock will grow to the former glory of the old. For many of these gardens there is now a need, albeit temporarily, to change the design emphasis with the construction of pergolas, summerhouses, dovecotes and trelliswork to fill the holes and provide new focal points.

In view of the fact that there are now large quantities of good quality timber available, it may well be worthwhile paying to have large sections of oak, cedar and pine planked and stored for use in future years.

Weathervane

Nowadays one rarely sees new weathervanes, although they are still made. This may be partly a reflection of our modern lifestyle – it is easy to imagine that in the days before satellite weather forecasting the weathervane was a very important indicator, to the gardener or labourer, of changes in the wind which heralded stormy, wet or cold weather. Now that we can glean this information in other ways, the weathervane is no longer even considered. Some houses are lucky enough to still have a weathervane, however, and very often it plays an important visual role. As an ornament, it can play the same role as, say, a lantern on a dome and provides a point of interest on an otherwise featureless surface. In the illustration the weathervane adds significantly to an ivy-covered wall – this particular example is considerably pock-marked from years of use as a target for air-rifle pellets.

A weathervane offers a delightful opportunity to commemorate some particular aspect of the local environment or community, in much the same way as would a village sign. It is nice to imagine, for example, a house on one of the great trout streams with a weathervane in the form of a fisherman landing his catch, or in Wimbledon, a tennis player serving an ace. Many readers will know of the cricketing weathervane that immortalises W. G. Grace. My only fear on this subject is that, inevitably, somebody will immortalise 'Cosy Nook' or 'Chez Nous' in the best tradition of Tack!

Covered Seat

One of the problems associated with the English garden is that, on the two days of summer, one is probably on holiday somewhere else and not able to sit out in the garden to enjoy it. The traditional answer to this has been the summerhouse or covered seat, tucked away in a sheltered corner.

The illustrated example is very simple in form, with a bench seat and attractive trellis screening allowing light into the structure. In a design sense the criticism of this structure could be that the roof is too flat, both in pitch and in texture. Dominated by the white trelliswork the seat presents a rather square appearance. A roof pitched at 35–40° with a good overhang, and either tiled or boarded, would balance the whole rather better. This is, however, nit-picking as by any standards it is an attractive item. The seat is placed in a rather interesting situation, actually set in a small annexe to the main garden and informally screened by hedging and a wisteria arch. Sitting in the seat one has a view through the arch to the main garden and classic Georgian house beyond.

Arched Bridge

This very attractive bridge illustrates perfectly the way in which a man-made structure can enhance the natural surroundings. Imagine this picture without the bridge. It would still be a lovely stretch of river, but lovely in a way that most would only notice fleetingly in an 'Oh look – that's a nice stretch of river' sort of way. The gentle curve of this well balanced bridge gives the view a focal point and makes a specific impression to the extent that, having once seen this view, one would always remember how nice it was – in the context of the bridge. 'Do you remember that lovely bridge over the river?' – the bridge becomes the vehicle by which one recalls the overall beauty of the scene. As I have previously mentioned, this, for me, is the essence of good design – that it adds to the environment!

The main bearing spans of this bridge are of unbroken lengths of pre-shaped timber, presumably bent in a steam and pressure process. The bearers are connected with wooden decking slats and uprights are bolted through bearers. The handrails are shorter lengths of timber spanning between uprights. The only drawback with this type of gently curving bridge is that for the unsuspecting person the surface can become quite treacherous in wet or icy weather.

Bench

Traditionally, the English garden bench was made of oak, one of the most durable of indigenous hardwoods. Its great strength and resistance to decay meant that it could be carved and worked into quite delicate sections while still retaining structural integrity. It could also be left in its natural condition without needing to worry about preservatives, which in any case were not available.

In recent years oak has largely been replaced by teak in the manufacture of garden benches. This oily hardwood is shipped in quantity from plantations in the Far East, owned and managed by the manufacturing companies in the UK. This arrangement provides cheap timber of consistent quality and section that lends itself well to commercial production techniques. The inevitable upshot is that an oak bench will certainly cost at least twice the price of a comparable article in teak. It is now very unusual to see any new oak garden furniture.

The two benches illustrated present an interesting contrast in design, style and presentation. The white bench is of a commercially manufactured design in teak. It has a very simple, clean design structure and represents the basic no-frills end of the market. The second bench is of oak and has a rather more 'worked' structure with interesting curves and shapes. It is more substantial in section and would have been part of a small production series.

In the sense of garden design the really interesting comparison between these two is in their presentation. The white-painted bench stands on its own on the lawn in much the same way as a statue would, and there is no attempt at discretion. The whiteness of the bench against the natural colours of lawn and trees allows it to play a very significant role in overall garden concept. The oak bench plays a more traditional design role. It is set against a background, the weathered colours of the timber blending with the surroundings in an undemanding way.

Which of these approaches is correct very much depends on the nature of the particular garden environment. Long stretches of lawn backed by trees or hedging may well benefit from a splash of white more than would the small cottage garden, where this degree of formality may be too distracting.

A word about painting benches! An oak bench should not be painted under any circumstances as paint will not adhere properly to the wood, very quickly cracking and peeling and allowing moisture to be trapped in the timber. This will eventually lead to decay. Good teak benches should not be painted for precisely the same reason, unless, as with the one illustrated, the wood is old and dry (not oily) and painting will improve its appearance and longevity. If you wish to paint an old teak bench do not use conventional oil-based painting systems but rather a microporous white-wood treatment such as Sadolin Pinotex Superdec. This treatment has a preservative action and its porosity will allow the wood to breathe to a certain extent, thus reducing the risk of deterioration through mould or other forms of decay. This form of treatment is also considerably easier to maintain in good condition.

Two different bench designs: (left) in teak; (right) in oak

Dovecotes

Historically the dovecote, or columbarium (*columba* being Latin for the large genus of pigeon) was an important food source, in much the same way as the fish pond (stew pond) was a managed resource. There are still a good number of surviving examples around the country, chiefly in large houses and stately homes. An established and contented pair of doves can breed up to three times a year with one, two or even three young from each hatching, and this provided a very useful quantity of meat for the table. Nowadays the dovecote is an ornamental structure and can play a very significant role in garden design. One of the construction projects in this book is a dovecote and various aspects of design and proportion are discussed in that section (see p.102). It may be useful to relate a story about dovecote design which, unfortunately, speaks volumes about the general inability of many people to perceive the difference between good and bad design.

Some while ago an article appeared in the local paper about a nursing home that had raised funds for a dovecote. I promptly sent them a photograph of the 'Cottage' dovecote (illustrated in construction section) on p.107, an attractive structure (although I am obviously biased!)

whose design and proportions would have suited the home well. The Matron of the nursing home thanked me for the information but said that she had already commissioned a local man to build the dovecote – presumably she had seen the plans for his dovecote and was happy with them. A year or so later I saw a picture of the finished article in the same local paper; it was quite hideous, being completely out of proportion, flat and badly designed. It was, however, heralded as a masterpiece. The moral of this story is that you can lead a horse to water but cannot make it drink!

The two dovecotes illustrated in this section represent the utilitarian end of the market. They are not fussy or complicated but are in proportion both in their construction and in their environments. The thatched dovecote is set among trees and tall bushes in an informal part of a secluded garden. There is no particular finesse to its manufacture but at least the roof pitch is in proportion to the supporting brackets and the main pole is of an appropriate section. One very often sees tiny dovecotes stuck on the top of 'telegraph poles'. The second dovecote is a smaller affair, but still retains a proportional balance in its design and construction and within the context of a small enclosed garden. It makes no pretence at being an important architectural feature but blends into the landscape subtly and pleasingly.

Dovecote variations: (left) the thatched version; (right) the small dovecote

Stone Seat

This piece is included for its singular charm and individuality. It is a curved stone seat set in an alcove along the terrace at Polesden Lacey in Surrey. As it happens it is neither particularly comfortable nor does it allow the sitter to enjoy the spectacular view from the terrace across the valley to the Ranmore woods beyond, since it is obstructed by a hedge on the other side of the terrace. What the seat does do is provide interest for the first time visitor – 'Oh look, isn't that a beautiful seat!' as he or she comes unexpectedly to the alcove; and it is a focus for future visits – 'I'll meet you at the stone seat down on the terrace'. In this way a simple stone seat, strategically positioned, plays many roles. It is practical, it is important to the design of the terrace, it is geographically important and, to my mind most importantly, it is one of the catalysts which we all need for remembering places and occasions. If my life depended on it I could not remember the particular contents of the many great houses I have visited, but I certainly do remember the stone seat at Polesden Lacey.

Design ideas: (below) the stone seat

(Right) the curved seat

Curved Seat

This piece has certainly seen better days but even in its present battered condition, it seems to me utterly charming. This is a bench for talking about politics, religion or philosophy with a close friend. It is very difficult to have a proper conversation with someone when you are both sitting on a normal garden bench and facing the same way. The tendency is for the words to somehow get lost or lose their weight as you gaze forward with half your mind on what is going on in the distance. A really heavyweight conversation needs two things – comfort and eye contact. A curved bench like this provides the opportunity for both and it is nice to think that the world may have been put to rights quite a few times from this bench.

In design terms it is difficult to imagine a more appropriate position, tucked as it is under the overhanging boughs of a tree and sheltered on either side by hedging and undergrowth. This situation provides the bench with a certain privacy and importance, to the extent that one can almost hear Mrs Jones saying to her son 'Don't disturb your father – he's sitting on his bench!' Given the right situation and views this is surely a classic design. The construction is quite straightforward and reference to the oak bench construction project on p.85 will provide most of the necessary information on materials and design. The weak point in this design are the three inner angles of the bench, and care needs to be taken to ensure the structural integrity and rigidity of the supporting framework at these points. The obvious material for the bench is oak, although a white-painted bench made from treated softwoods would be most attractive in many gardens, the whiteness of the piece being potentially very useful in garden design.

Trellised Porch

This attractive trellised porch illustrates quite clearly how a very simple structure, provided that it is properly and sympathetically designed, can play a role out of all proportion to its cost or practical usefulness.

The obvious feature of this pretty cottage is the gothic shape of the windows and door. The porch has been built to reflect this shape and it does so in a strong, unfussy way that serves to further enhance the shape of the cottage. The other significant factor (which cannot be appreciated in the black and white photograph) is its colour – a strong red, which sets very effectively against the white cottage.

The use of colour can often make the difference between good or bad design, and can sometimes reduce the visual effectiveness of good structural design. If, for example, this porch were painted white it would, of course, remain attractive but it would no longer retain the visual importance bestowed on it by the present colour, particularly when viewed against the white walls. Alternatively, the porch could have been painted in a colour entirely unsympathetic to its surroundings – the strong red used is actually complementary to the greens of the hedge and the white behind whereas some yellows, for example, would not be.

A useful exercise for anybody wishing to select a colour for a particular purpose is to go to a good art materials shop which sells the full range of 'Magic Markers' (spirit-based markers). Each colour is divided into ten or more shades ranging from the 'cold' side of a colour to the 'hot' side. Once a designer appreciates the range and nature of shades of colour he will never again just think of colour simply in terms of light or dark.

Summerhouse

This illustration is actually of a pay-booth at the entrance to Ickworth (National Trust) in Suffolk. It does, however, represent a classic style of wooden summerhouse. This one is attractive in many respects but particularly in the proportion of its roof, and is a good example of how a 'tall' garden requires 'tall' garden furniture (see p.7). The steeply pitched roof (nominally 50°), embellished with a sharp, turned post, is superbly suited to its position among tall trees. In a summerhouse role this structure would

certainly benefit from the installation of double French doors, spanning two sides of the octagonal shape and allowing uninterrupted views from a sofa or comfortable chairs. This format, combined with an electricity supply for light, heat and the kettle, would make it an ideal all-seasons' hideaway at the end of anybody's garden.

The construction of such a summerhouse is quite straightforward provided that sufficient attention is paid to the establishment of the supporting framework. Ideally the major supporting upright timbers should be concreted into the ground and securely tied and braced at ceiling level, to guard against movement during gales. There is a great tendency for relatively small structures like this to 'twist' in the wind, and this can have devastating consequences, particularly when clad with extremely heavy tiled roofs.

The Opportunity for Experiment

What would you say the thatched structure illustrated actually was? A summerhouse? a pergola? some sort of folly? In fact it is a bridge above a road driven through a deep cutting. The designer was obviously aware that a simple bridge would suffice but saw an opportunity to build something a little more elaborate that would serve other purposes as well. The structure born from his opportunism is probably unique both in its design and its range of uses. It is both a bridge, a summerhouse and a high seat, with very interesting views looking back to a formal garden, onwards to meadowland, and down to the road beneath which at the time of the bridge's manufacture would have been an important local cart-track and thoroughfare.

This is a singular structure built for a singular position but it has wider value as an illustration of just how much scope for experiment and enterprise there can be in the design and manufacture of garden furniture. If you are lucky enough to have an interesting and expansive garden why feel constrained to install merely 'ordinary' garden furniture, that can only ever be utilitarian. Why not take a wider view of the whole and consider whether it is possible to design and build something just a little special, or even unique?

Although it does not relate to garden furniture I came across a good example of the desire to experiment and innovate with design at a house near Croydon. The large garden of the house lay along a terrace, halfway up a steep hillside with the land rising up from the left-hand side and falling away to the right. Towards the end of the garden was a beautiful pond, perhaps 50ft (15m) across, teeming with plant and fish life. The setting for the pond was quite perfect and when I began to congratulate the owner he pointed out that it was actually artificial. I realised then that no natural pond could exist in such a position on the hillside, but this only made its creation more admirable. He had thought 'That would be a marvellous place for a pond' and he had then set about making it. In the same way I would recommend the creation of much garden furniture, whether it be a bench, summerhouse, bridge or pergola. Build for design rather than just for use.

The opportunity for experiment – build for design as well as use

Formal Perspective

This photograph illustrates one view of the formal gardens at Polesden Lacey, Surrey, and shows very clearly the contribution that garden furniture can make to a garden plan.

It is interesting to consider how gardens of this type came to be built, and to draw comparisons with the development of the modern garden. Having received the instruction to plan a formal garden the architect would first have considered the boundaries and how these would be defined, and then the perspective of views of – and through – the garden. His first jottings would have included the type and height of walls, the style of gates into the gardens, the latticework of paths through the garden and the statuary and ornament that would complement these paths and views together. Only when this basic structural framework had been developed would the planner have considered what plants should be grown – these would add to the structural plan and be dominated by it. The boxed hedges in the illustration, for example, reflect and continue the formal theme established by the gate pillars. Roses and other flowers would also have been planted in formal groupings of colour and style so as to reflect other aspects of the overall structural formality.

The emphasis, therefore, was very much on the creation of a garden around a carefully planned and built permanent infrastructure of garden furniture. You may feel that the use of the term 'garden furniture' is rather too broad in this instance. It is not, for example, the accepted terminology for a garden gate but call it what you may, the fact is that a gate such as this has no purpose other than as 'garden furniture'. Without the garden the gate need not exist, as it was designed and built solely to define the garden and be part of it. This is my interpretation of the rôle of garden furniture.

The establishment of a modern garden usually follows a rather different course. Planning centres around the use of plants, trees and lawns to create interesting formal and informal views and perspectives, and where garden furniture is introduced it is usually as an optional extra which will enable the gardener to enjoy the garden in comfort, or help the display of climbing plants. Obviously, any comparison between the great houses and the ordinary small garden can never be entirely valid as there are just too many differences in opportunity and environment. I believe, however, that it will certainly benefit the garden planner to consider the structural framework of his or her garden rather more, and at an earlier stage, than presently seems to be the case.

The formal gardens at Polesden Lacey in Surrey

2 The New England Garden

Although this book is primarily concerned with the English country garden I felt that it would be interesting and instructive to look at what other countries had to offer in the way of garden furniture. I was drawn to look at the New England states of the USA, primarily because I had a 'picture-postcard' image of this area in the fall and felt that it would be similar to the British Isles in more than name only. I went to New England expecting to find a mirror image of what I was used to at home. This was not the case at all. As far as I could tell the area known as New England comprises the states of Connecticut, Massachusetts, Rhode Island, New Hampshire, Vermont and Maine. My journey took me to Connecticut, Massachusetts, Rhode Island, New York state and the tri-state area of New York, Pennsylvania and New Jersey. For the purposes of this book I have taken the liberty of temporarily expanding New England to include these latter areas.

It very quickly became apparent to me that the average American garden, at least in this part of the country, is completely unlike the average British garden. For one thing the scale is different – whereas a suburban or rural house plot in the British Isles is likely to be about 1/10th of an acre (.04ha), with anything over ¼ acre (.10ha) being considered large, in New England an ordinary plot is between 1 and 3 acres (.4 and 1.2ha). The other very interesting factor is the style of house-building. Whereas in the UK houses are usually built on level ground, or ground that has been levelled, in New England the houses are often built on substantial timber or steel foundations which pay no heed to the natural topography. This means that many houses are built into steep wooded banks without any particular need to level out the usually hilly terrain. This combination of space and position, coupled with the extreme natural beauty of the environment, makes it both impractical and unnecessary to garden in the way we know it.

Anyone for a swim?; (inset) a timber and steel bridge

26

Broadly the New England garden may be described as trees with lawns. More accurately the description should read beautiful trees on beautiful lawns in a beautiful landscape. Although there are shrubs and flowers of some sort in most gardens, these pale into insignificance against the scale and completeness of the garden landscapes. The New England houses are nearly always derived from the colonial house styles of the eighteenth and nineteenth centuries (although these days the wood is quite likely to be vinyl) which complement the gardens perfectly and, in particular, the fall colours.

In New England I looked for interesting items of garden furniture to photograph but at first found it very hard to find anything that I considered worthwhile. This was mainly because I had mistakenly expected to find the same things as in the UK, perhaps designed in some slightly different way; but eventually, I realised that, to the New Englander, the most important part of the garden is the 'deck' or verandah. The deck is a raised wooden structure which provides a level extension to the ground floor providing, in effect, a raised patio. It is on this deck, or on the front verandah in some of the more substantial colonial homes, that the New Englander sits, Budweiser in hand, to contemplate the garden or entertain his guests. For most people the deck, with a few chairs and a table, is the only garden furniture needed or even considered. There are, nevertheless, some gardens which give greater prominence to other garden furniture and generally this is in keeping with the colonial tradition and in proportion to the environment.

Garden Fence

This photograph was taken in the town of New Hope, Pennsylvania, an extremely attractive town in the Delaware valley north of Philadelphia – and this is the most attractive garden fence that I have ever seen, particularly set as it is against clap-board houses in the colonial style. There are several factors contributing to the success of this fence and it is useful to consider these in turn.

Shape – without the raised posts and staggered palings this fence would be very nice, but ordinary, and the photograph would have been essentially of two straight lines like a railway track. By adding raised posts and staggering the palings up to them, the eye is drawn to the detail of the fence which instead of just being ordinary becomes an architectural piece in its own right. The importance of the work is further emphasised by the dominant newel posts on either side of the centrally positioned gate.

Detail – the shape of the structure is enhanced by the details of construction and, in particular, by the careful pointing of each upright paling. This detail achieves a particular importance when, as in the photograph, strong evening sunlight catches the points and creates very interesting contrasts of light and dark.

Construction – this is extremely good in every sense, and particularly as:

- The only timbers in ground contact are the pressure-treated posts.
- Fence rails are jointed into posts, rather than just laid-on.
- Palings are substantial square sections of timber (1½× 1½in (38×38mm)) rather than slats.

Colour – the obvious and correct choice is white. A formal fence of this quality should always be painted white, as it is only this colour that will emphasise its importance, while at the same time complementing the natural colours around it. Were this same fence painted black or brown it would lose a great deal of its identity as a result. Had this been the case I doubt whether it would have caught my eye and this book would not have been graced by its presence.

Ranch fencing technique

A rather elegant garden fence design

Trellised Porch

In the New England landscape there is nothing very unusual about this sort of porch, and there is certainly nothing difficult about its manufacture or installation. This particular example represents the ideal design and use for a trellised framework. Imagine the same house without the trellised porch. It would still be very attractive but the door would be ordinary, the house front would be far less interesting and the predominant white of board cladding would tend to flatten the overall effect.

A different idea for the trellised porch

With the trellised porch the front door assumes a new identity. It becomes welcoming – the sort of place where you would feel comfortable when greeting friends or chatting to neighbours. The doorway also becomes visually important, the eye being drawn to the porch area, and this effect also serves to add interest to the rest of the house front, particularly through the creation of shadows. The illustrated porch is most impressive in its proportion, neither too obtrusive nor too flimsy. It provides useful shelter for the door area yet its airy structure does not intrude, and the trellis provides an ideal climbing frame for plants – it is easy to imagine a beautiful clematis or rose climbing through the trelliswork and upwards to the roof.

Square Summerhouse

I suspect that this summerhouse, set as it is in the grounds of an eighteenth-century colonial mansion, was built at a time when money was not a problem to the owner. Sadly, it is difficult to imagine many people today who would be prepared to pay the price required for such a highly worked structure, particularly in England where the weather would limit the number of days it could be used in the average year. I am not even sure how a carpenter would go about producing some of the components required, in particular the rounded corner posts which presumably have been worked on a lathe able to accept 10ft (3m) lengths of timber.

The structure is an interesting exercise in proportion and design, with the designer turning what could have been a very destructive square shape into a far more sympathetic form by using rounded posts, ornate wrought- or cast-iron brackets and by careful positioning and scale of roof and rails. Its situation in the grounds of the property is quite correct for its particular purpose, which was as an annexe to the wide verandah of a colonial home – it would be equally correct as the focal point of an extremely large garden, placed at the end of a long pathway at some distance from the property and backed by tall trees. It may be useful to consider the main elements of design and construction:

The Roof The 'shingle' roof is quite common in many applications in the United States, where appropriate types and sections of timber are readily available; shingles are sometimes found in England and would normally be of oak. The principle of this form of roof covering is that thin wooden panels are laid with the grain running vertically so that water will run with the grain of wood on its way to the ground in much the same way as it would follow the individual straws of a thatched roof. Shingles are laid and overlapped in the same way as plain tiles or slates and, if looked after, can last for many years. For most rigid structural garden furniture shingles would be the ideal

roofing, being both effective and sympathetic to the garden landscape. An important feature of this summerhouse is the ornamental roof embellishment in the form of a spike, which draws the eye upwards and effectively elongates the structure, helping to soften its squareness as well as providing an attractive finish to the whole structure.

Brackets The spectacular cast- or wrought-iron brackets joining corner posts to roof bearers are very significant both visually and structurally. They lead the eye gently from the strong lines of the corner posts to the broad expanse of roof – without these brackets the eye would be forced to stop at the top of the posts, before jumping to the roof; with them, the posts and roof become one structure. It is almost inconceivable that brackets such as these could be produced economically for one summerhouse, unless you happen to know an old blacksmith who would do it for very little. It is more likely that anyone wishing to emulate this design feature will end up searching fruitlessly through piles of second-hand building materials. However, a very attractive wooden alternative may be seen on the octagonal summerhouse illustrated on p.33.

Corner Posts These magnificent rounded and decorated posts have an intricate visual effect on the summerhouse. They are squared at the base and roof, providing strong sections of timber for jointing with brackets and rails, and are rounded for most of their length, creating an effect of lightness. Colour also plays an important role, with the rounded sections being made even less obtrusive with the application of white paint.

Banister Rails The quality and intricate construction of these components is obvious and admirable. In a design sense it seems to me that the most important aspect of this part of the structure is its height, or lack of it. The banister rails are very low (about 28in (70cm)) and serve merely to define the floor area, rather than to create a closed space. The lowness and lightness of the assembly adds to the feeling of space and elegance given by the summerhouse.

(*overleaf*) Summerhouse designs: (left) square and (right) octagonal

Octagonal Summerhouse

This beautiful summerhouse is garden furniture at its very best. It is perfectly proportioned and designed and the manufacturer has gone to great lengths to finish the product to a very high standard. The two things that are disappointing are its position (alongside a busy road and therefore hardly conducive to its use as a quiet hideaway) and its unstained finish, the wood being left in the 'green' treated state. The structure is made entirely of pressure-treated (tanalised) timbers (softwood), and has a shingled roof. It embodies a great many very attractive and interesting design features.

Supporting posts These posts are lengths of 3×3in (75× 75mm) softwood timber, slightly chamfered, boxed with 4in (100mm) plank at the base and (partially) top. The design effect of this boxing is to reduce the visual impact of the posts for much of their length. You may wish to compare this feature with the slightly different technique employed in the square summerhouse on p.31.

Brackets and 'ladderwork' above Again, brackets are employed both to assist structural rigidity and to draw the eye gently from the supporting posts up towards the roof. They are made of nicely decorated softwood but do not lead directly to the roof, but rather via a 'ladderwork' structure reflecting the handrail below. This very attractive and unusual feature, when combined with the arch created by the brackets, provides the most visually important element of the whole structure. You may test this yourself by simply looking at the picture and noting where your eye is drawn.

Shingled roof The problems associated with multi-facet structures are legion, and I am particularly impressed with the neatness of this roof. Constructed of shingles laid onto exterior ply, itself laid onto a framework of rafters, the roof is finished with an attractive fascia board 'laid-back' towards the structure. The way that the fascia reclines is, in itself, a very useful device, serving to blend the roof into the lower structure.

The Lantern Consider how easy it would have been to finish the roof with a knob or spike, rather than this highly intricate and beautifully designed lantern. It is a pro-portional mirror-image of the summerhouse itself. The visual purpose of a lantern is actually to give balance to a large expanse of roof, although it may also be a structural device serving (as in the case of St. Paul's Cathedral in London) to weigh down the top of a dome, preventing any extraneous movement in the structure.

The Floor Another attractive feature of this summerhouse is the careful design of the internal floor, the boards being laid on bearers to create eight triangular segments. This style of construction is appropriate for a floor laid directly to the ground, but would not necessarily be correct for a suspended floor which requires some contribution to structural rigidity from the spanning floorboards.

Colour This summerhouse has been left in the 'green', pressure-treated state, but I feel that it deserves better than this and should be coloured with a combination of opaque white-wood treatment and wood stains. Use of colour would serve to emphasise the formal qualities of the summerhouse construction whereas, left in the raw, it tends to withdraw into the landscape. If I were lucky enough to own this summerhouse, I would want it to be a very significant feature in the garden.

Deck

Although there is nothing very attractive about either the house or the environment illustrated in this photograph, it provides a clear picture of the standard 'deck' to be found in many homes. While in New England I gradually came to sympathise with this sort of structure, which offers an extremely convenient and practical opportunity to extend the living area of a house into the garden. Deck structures are particularly useful in properties where the land falls steeply away from the house, offering the chance to create quite spectacular raised structures jutting out over steep valleys and cliffs. It is certainly an idea which should be applied in the UK, and I can personally think of at least half-a-dozen properties that would be greatly enhanced with a sensitively designed deck.

Modern decks are constructed entirely from pressure-treated (tanalised) timber. Substantial softwood posts (6in (15cm) dia) are secured into concrete foundations and a supporting framework built up from these. Floor planking is generally of 6–7×1½in (15–18×3.8cm) softwood plank, secured with galvanised nails. The main construction can be clearly seen in the illustration. As with all garden furniture and architecture, the deck can be an acute visual embarrassment unless designed very carefully. The illustrated example is most attractive, with the vertical palings and well proportioned staircase helping to create a pleasingly formal structure. Many decks are rather less well designed, with haphazard trellis work, rustic poles etc. Often the timber is left in the green treatment colour, which can be pleasing, but does not sit well against the neat decoration of most New England homes.

Garden Shed

The most usual and utilitarian item of garden furniture in both the New and Old Worlds is undoubtedly the garden shed. The normal design of the New England shed is as shown in the illustration, with a two-part chalet roof looking Flemish in design, though individual products vary greatly in quality and dimension, with this particular example representing the good end of the range. Interestingly it is normal to receive delivery of these sheds ready-made and this, as much as anything else, emphasises the fundamental difference between the US and the UK: SPACE! How many British gardens could receive a substantial article like this – in one piece?

On both sides of the Atlantic, the garden shed offers unparallelled opportunity for the expression of bad taste – whereas in the UK my complaint would be of meanness of design and inferior materials, in the US it would be reserved for vinyl roof tiles in gaudy colours. The vinyl roof is an accepted part of their architecture and most factory-built houses have a vinyl-tile roof as standard, but the manufacturers seem to keep the most obtrusive ones in reserve for garden sheds. In fact, compared with mineral felt, vinyl roof tiles are tough, durable and, providing the colour is reasonable, can look texturally very effective once laid, as the illustrated example clearly shows. The tiles are stuck on to flat, exterior-ply boards laid over conventional rafter systems. I did, however, see a number of properties with roof tiles curling up at the corners, like rather old sandwiches, so there is obviously an art to proper installation.

Swinging Seat

This very simple and attractive seat was one of only a very few formal garden seats that I saw in New England. The normal garden seating is very much of the plastic and metal patio variety, or wooden slatted seats of basic form. Apart from the odd bench in public areas there seems to be very little traditional, crafted bench seating. This is not surprising given that the social emphasis is around the patio or deck rather than the lawn.

The construction of this seat is fairly straightforward, with slats morticed into upper and lower back rails etc, though the back reclines quite steeply for comfort. It is for

the individual to work out a system for hanging such a seat but, in this case, it is doubtful if the supporting chains have been correctly positioned or installed. It might have been safer if the chains had been secured to the seat-bearing timbers, so that these bore all the loads applied to the seat during use. Instead they are secured to the armrest assembly with the effect that all the joints in the structure must be significantly stressed during use. Furthermore, the chain configuration seems inappropriate in that the seat would have to stay in one position for the load to be spread evenly to the four anchor points. A large man, leaning far

back into the seat, would undoubtedly tip the seat backwards transferring all the load to just two anchor points. One way round this problem may be to replace the lower part of the chains with a strong 'elastic' that will serve to equalise the loads between front and rear anchors. Nonetheless I was impressed with the thought behind this seat, and with its position. My further consideration, as someone who is forever moving benches around the garden to get them out of the way of the lawnmower, is that hanging benches could be quite a good labour-saving device!

Rustic Pergola

On the whole, I am not a fan of rustic garden furniture, but this example represents an overall attempt at formal garden symmetry which is something rarely seen in the New England garden. The scene is attractive – steps leading through symmetrical borders up to the symmetrical and central pergola structure, although personally I would prefer to see the pergola made with properly prepared and treated timbers and covered with climbing plants. How-ever, those who like the rustic style will appreciate the following features:

Scale The pergola is very large, looking as though it is meant to be there, and is set at the end of a long view where it is given scale and perspective by the background of tall trees and by the tall firs that bracket it in the foreground.

Design The pergola is put together in a recognisable form and, in the context of the whole garden, has a clearly defined role as a place to go to for drinks before dinner etc. It is light and airy, allowing uninterrupted views to the rest of the garden.

An elaborate rustic pergola; (below) a more ornate pergola/gazebo

Lakeside Pavilion

This lakeside pavilion is definitely garden furniture on the grand scale. Although I have some reservations about the design, it seems to me that this particular structure makes the most of a natural feature in a very satisfying way. It acts as a bridge, a summerhouse and a barbecue and it also achieves the primary purpose of good garden furniture or architecture by 'adding' to the environment – in other words, it draws the attention of the passer-by to itself, and to the surrounding area of water, trees and lawn and the uniform reaction is 'Doesn't that look beautiful!', or words to that effect. Without the pavilion the scene would not attract the same interest or comment, it would simply be yet another pretty picture in a sea of pretty New England pictures.

The practical design is extremely effective, but it would seem that the roof, and roof supports, are not quite in keeping with the base. It is useful to refer to the square summerhouse on p.32 for some design comparisons. With the summerhouse a great effort was made to reduce the impact of the supporting posts by removing their 'squareness' and blending them in to the roof structure using attractive and carefully shaped brackets. In this pavilion the supporting posts are visually dominant and there is a clash between the gentle curve and careful construction of the handrail assembly and the very strong lines of posts and roof. To soften this harsh effect, the following could be done: replace the very strong brackets at the top of the posts with something less substantial, chamfer the posts to remove a degree of their squareness, and soften the line of the roof by removing the white 'stripe' of the fascia board, replacing it with a wood stain of appropriate colour. This would move the visual emphasis down to the very attractive handrail assembly, and its reflection in the water.

Although I know nothing of the history of this project I would not be surprised to learn that the platform was built first, followed at a later stage by the roof. This would certainly explain the apparent contrast of styles. This photograph was taken in Fairfield County, Connecticut – a beautiful area.

Martin House

In New England there is a great interest in attracting and feeding the bird population. Normally, as in the UK, this interest expresses itself in the form of bird tables and hanging feeders. Occasionally you may see a martin house designed to attract a nesting population – this particular model was photographed in Dutchess County, New York State.

A beautiful lakeside pavilion
(Inset) a variation on the British dovecote: a martin house

Gazebo

The wedding photographer's dream! – a wrought-iron gazebo, on an island in the middle of a small lake! And that is precisely the use for this particularly well proportioned and attractive structure.

I am in two minds about the role of this type of highly worked, ornate and formal structure in the English garden. I feel that its design role should be as a far-away viewpoint – at the end of a very long stretch of landscaped and formal lawn, and close to water. The structure shrieks formality and represents late Victorian garden planning at its most obvious. It is very easy to imagine such a structure surrounded by Victorian ladies with parasols, and tail-coated gentlemen. The gazebo represents the best expression of the craft of wrought-ironwork – the curves and intricate shapes of the structure could not be reproduced in wood without becoming heavy and obtrusive, and the cost would be enormous. As it is, a wrought-iron gazebo of this quality would itself cost a small fortune.

Garden Chair

This attractive, comfortable and simple design is very common in New England in both single and double seat format. The construction is fairly obvious from the illustration, with all loads being transferred to the joints securing vertical legs to angled seat bearers. These joints are very securely bolted to prevent movement. Loads from the seat back are transferred through armrests to legs and thus to bolted joints. The chairs are constructed from treated softwood (nominally 4×1in $(10 \times 2.5$cm) finished thickness) and the design obviates the need for large sections of timber that would normally be used in upright benches.

The only cautionary note would be that older, less agile people might get well and truly stuck in the steeply reclining seat!

(Left) the gazebo; (below) wooden garden chair

Rustic Swinging Chair

This chair is included for general interest since some readers may feel the design appropriate for particular garden applications. The structure is quite hideous and it may be a useful design exercise to compare it with the swinging seat illustrated on p.37.

The rustic swinging chair

Twenty-first Century Garden Furniture

This photograph is included mainly because it depicts so beautifully the character of New England – superb houses, clear air, water and trees! The house is actually in the Delaware Valley, Pennsylvania, so not strictly New England, the water being part of the (now disused) Delaware Navigation Canal. The picture also holds the main element of the twenty-first century town planners' nightmare – a satellite dish. In this instance the dish is discreetly positioned, low down and next to the house, and is itself attractively designed; the blend of modern technology with classic house and garden is interesting and attractive, or at least acceptable. This certainly was not the case with many such dishes. Most seemed to be about ten feet across (3m) and completely overpowered both house and garden in the most monstrously obtrusive and ill-considered way.

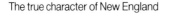

The true character of New England

3 General Construction Principles

Multi-facet Structures

It is vital, in the sectional construction of many of the projects in this book, to angle wall and roof frames so that each will fit precisely to the next, giving a robust and cohesive assembly. Illustrations in each of the project chapters will give a broad idea of what is required in principle and the following information will provide you with the precise angles needed for each type of assembly. All the angles given are accurate to one decimal point. In practice you will be lucky to cut to anything like this accuracy, and the odd degree will not matter too much. You should, however, really aim for precision, if only to ensure that your overall result will be satisfactory.

> ### WALL FRAME ANGLES
> This is the angle of each frame section to the cladding which it supports.
> 8-sided structures: 22.5° (2×22.5°=45°)
> – the actual inside angle of each corner)
> 6-sided structures: 30° (2×30°=60°)
> – the actual angle of each corner)
> The formula is very simple:
> Angle of frame to panel = 360° ÷ Number of frame pieces.
>   *ie* 360° ÷ 16 (8-sided) = 22.5°
>   360° ÷ 12 (6-sided) = 30°

Roof Sections (This is the tricky bit!)
In many of the projects octagonal (or hexagonal) roofs, coming to a single apex, are made through the assembly of identical triangular panels, each of which has a *'pitch'* and a frame angled to fit the next frame at that given pitch. This principle will be clear to you after reference to Fig 1 which shows the essential elements involved.

Tables giving the most useful frame and apex angles are shown here, along with the rather complex formulae needed to obtain them. These formulae may not mean a lot to you but I include them if only because this is probably the first time that formulae relating to this type of construction have been published in a useful form. As far as I know these angles have previously been established by trial and error. If any reader wishes to know more about the proving of either formula I will be happy to assist.

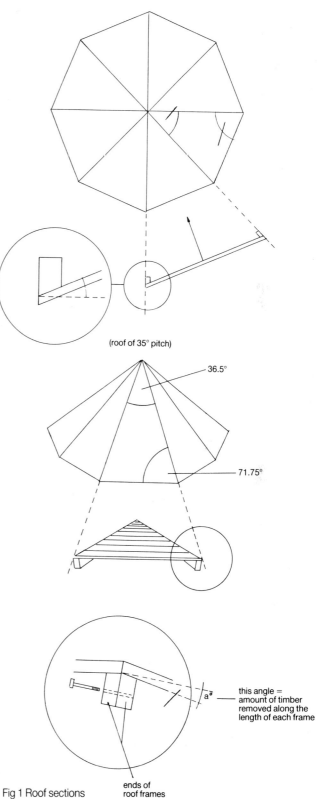

(roof of 35° pitch)

36.5°

71.75°

a°

this angle = amount of timber removed along the length of each frame

ends of roof frames

Fig 1 Roof sections

Octagonal Base (8 sides)	Roof Pitch	Apex°	Frame°
	30°	38.7°	9.9°
	35°	36.5°	13.4°
	40°	34.1°	14.9°

Hexagonal Base (6 sides)	Roof Pitch	Apex°	Frame°
	30°	51.3°	16.1°
	35°	48.4°	18.3°
	40°	45.0°	20.4°

Formula to ascertain *apex* angle for any given pitch of roof.

Where $\theta = 90°$ – angle of pitch and n is the number of sides of the base (or number of triangles used).

$$2 \sin^{-1} (\sin (\frac{180}{n}) \sin \theta)$$

Formula to ascertain *frame* angle (angle 'a' Fig 1)

Where $\theta = 90°$ – angle of pitch and n is the number of sides of the base (or number of triangles used)

$$90° - \sin^{-1} \frac{\sin (\frac{90 (n-2)}{n})}{\sqrt{1 - \sin^2 \theta \, \sin^2 (\frac{180}{n})}}$$

Explanation of angle 'a': In a roof designed with x-segments (hexagonal, octagonal etc), each roof frame must have timber trimmed from along the length of its 'top' face, so that when the roof cladding is in place and the roof assembled, the completed roof segments fit snugly together. Angle 'a' indicates the amount of timber to be removed.

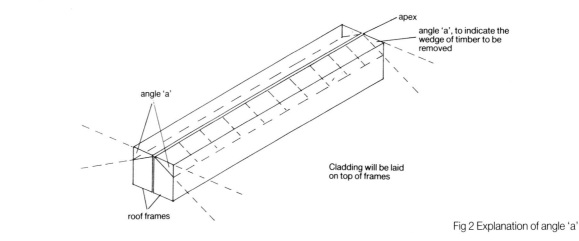

Fig 2 Explanation of angle 'a'

Jig and Template Construction

In projects requiring the accurate reproduction of particular components a jig or template of some form should generally be used. The role of a jig, for the purposes of this book, is to provide a rigid and accurate frame in which to assemble and finish a particular set of components. Templates are used generally for marking out purposes and are used here to guide tools being used in the production of components.

Template 1. Timber cladding for walls

This template is required for the summerhouse and dovecote projects; with it you are endeavouring to mass-produce lengths of tongue and groove or shiplap timber of an exact length and with precisely angled cut surfaces. The principle is that you provide a rigid surface against which you can run a circular saw *ie* cutting timber held in the template. Fig 3 describes such a template. The angle of cut will depend on the number of sides to the finished structure and you should refer to Angles for Multi-facet

Structures for guidance. It is absolutely vital to get the angles correct and consistent.

Procedure:

1 Provide a large, flat, firm surface on which to construct the template. A sheet of 12mm chipboard (1220mm× 2440mm) is ideal for most purposes. (This material will be damaged during construction so it is not a bad idea to ask your timber merchants if they have any damaged stock they could sell you cheaply.)

2 With reference to Fig 3 fix a guide batten (A) to the lower edge of your board; drill through the chipboard and screw into the batten (sometimes spelled baton) if you are not using the special chipboard screws now available. This batten should be of the same thickness as the wood you will be cutting, so that the saw can run across it easily.

3 Decide how many pieces of timber you wish to cut on each stroke and lay this number (tongues in groove or lapped) against the base guide, external faces uppermost (B).

4 Secure a straight, strong batten (C) across the timber *precisely* 90° to the run of the wood and a few inches in from

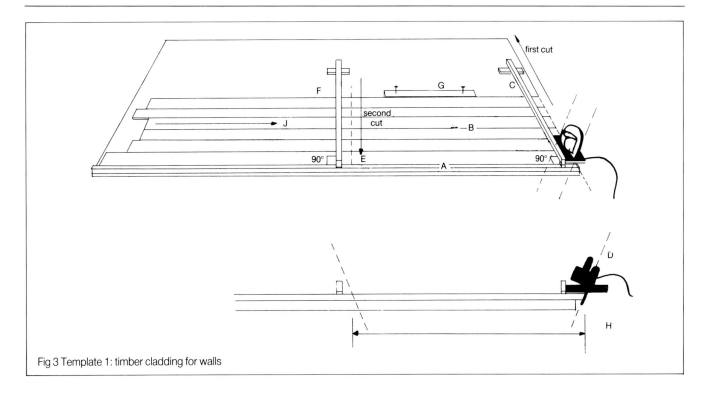

Fig 3 Template 1: timber cladding for walls

the right-hand edge of the chipboard (pack this batten slightly so that it does not actually rest on the object timber). Position this batten so that the saw blade does not cut into your board.

5 Set your circular saw to the correct angle (D), run it against the batten (C) and cut slightly into the base guide (A).

6 Measure the required length of timber from this test cut and mark it (E). Paying particular attention to the

Fig 4 Using a template to prepare side-frame cladding

direction of travel indicated in Fig 2 assess the position of saw guide (F). Secure this guide as with C (it does not matter which side of F your saw travels along).

7 Secure another guide (G) at the top of the template so as to secure the pieces being worked, but not so tightly that nothing can move.

8 Set your circular saw to such a depth that you will cut through the object wood and *slightly* into the template board surface (H).

9 Double check your measurements and, if all is all right, cut a sample piece by running the saw *up* the first guide (right-hand side) and *down* the second guide. You must always work in this circular motion to ensure the correct angles.

10 Cut further pieces and move timber to be cut along the template as required (J). Always ensure that the saw is held firmly against the guides and that you are well past the work before withdrawing the blade.

11 Stack the cut pieces in the order in which they are cut.

> **NOTES**
> In a workshop with limited space it will be important to buy timber in relatively short lengths. If this is the case make sure that these lengths are divisible by the length of the finished component – otherwise you will end up with a lot of kindling!
>
> Keep checking that the angle of the circular saw is correct. Some saws are very awkward to fix at an angle and have the habit of working loose.

Template 2. A system for preparing wall/roof frames
The sectional construction described through the major projects in this book requires the accurate production of frames cut along their length to the correct angle; to which cladding panels are then applied, for wall and roof constructions. It is particularly important that these angles should be accurate and the following practical system will help.

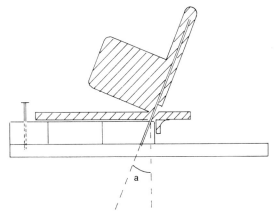

Fig 5 Wall/roof frame preparation

Procedure:
1 With reference to Fig 5 lay a batten along the long edge of your work surface and secure it with screws or nails. Ensure that the fixings do not stand proud of the wood.
2 Lay a number of pieces of the timber to be cut along this batten so that you provide a firm level bed along which the circular saw may travel.
3 Set the saw to the appropriate angle (see Multi-facet Structures p.47) and set the saw guide as in Fig 5. Cutting depth should be set fractionally over what is required.

Angle (a) shown in Fig 5 is the same angle shown in Fig 1. This procedure should be used for production of both wall and roof frames – the only difference being the angle of cut.
4 Either move the saw along the object wood *or*, if you have assistance, move the wood through the saw. The latter method could be dangerous to the inexperienced: be careful to keep the saw firmly in position along the cut, and particularly at the end. For safety, if you are pushing object wood through the saw use a push stick at the end of the length, rather than bring your fingers close to the blade.

Jig 1. Construction and use of jig for assembly of side and wall sections (summerhouse, dovecote)
The role of this jig is to provide a rigid and accurate frame in which the parts manufactured using Templates 1 and 2 may be assembled. The size of the jig, and its angles, will vary and you should use timber of large enough section to ensure rigidity for the particular project in hand.

Procedure:
If there is any uncertainty about this procedure it will be helpful to look at the photographs illustrating the dovecote project (see p.102). These show the jig in use.

This chapter should be read in the context of the particular structure you wish to produce, as there is a marked difference in scale between projects and one or two specific differences in manufacture. In the summerhouse project, for example, it is necessary to pre-drill bolt holes to connect finished wall panels. A plan of this is given in this section, and a more comprehensive explanation in the text of the summerhouse project.

1 To make the jig, use the method shown in Template 2 to prepare two lengths of timber (as long as the panel to be produced), by cutting a wedge of the same degree and length as the frame to be assembled from each length. Retain the cut wedges which will become components (i) and (ii) in Fig 6b. The degree of cut will obviously depend on the type of structure being made, and will already have been assessed in the production of side-frame components in Template 2. Fix one of the prepared pieces at 90° to a straight edge of your work surface or base board as shown in Fig 6. Fix a wedge alongside it as shown in Fig 6b (i). By doing this you are creating a 'cradle' for the components to sit in during assembly. Unless you intend to cut cladding in situ (as with pergola roof sections) the side pieces (Fig 6c C) should finish higher than the articles to be assembled (Fig 6c, A and F) so that cladding will be held firm within the jig.
2 Assess the correct position for the second part of the jig by laying frame and cladding components onto fixed side, and butting remaining jig pieces up to the components until an accurate position may be established. Ensure that the second jig side is precisely equidistant from first side along its entire length, and that it is at 90° to the base. Secure jig and double-check for accuracy before use. Refer to dovecote Fig 5 for jig in use.
3 Fig 6a shows the intended fitting of one finished frame section to another and, by studying this, you will realise importance of accuracy at this stage. This figure also shows the line of pre-drilled bolt holes that will be necessary to secure summerhouse wall sections together.
4 Once the completed jig has been checked for accuracy, secure a length of batten along the base (Fig 6c, E) to act as a downward stop for frame and cladding components being introduced to the jig.

Using the wall section jig
1 Before you start wall section assembly read and understand the section in Multi-facet Structures relating to angles in the wall frames to reflect roof pitch (see p.47). If making a summerhouse, also refer to the summerhouse

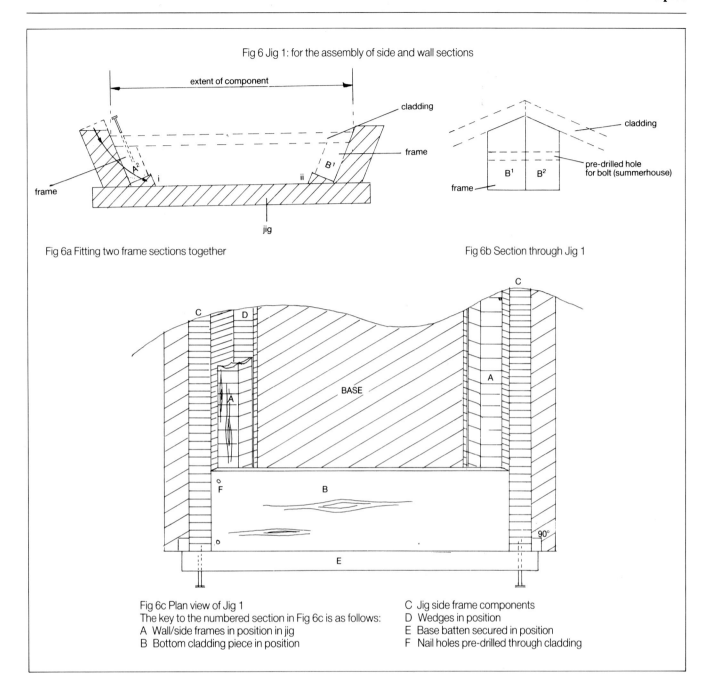

Fig 6 Jig 1: for the assembly of side and wall sections

extent of component

cladding

frame

frame

A²

i

ii

B¹

jig

Fig 6a Fitting two frame sections together

cladding

frame

B¹ B²

pre-drilled hole
for bolt (summerhouse)

Fig 6b Section through Jig 1

C

D

C

A

A

BASE

F

B

E

90°

Fig 6c Plan view of Jig 1
The key to the numbered section in Fig 6c is as follows:
A Wall/side frames in position in jig
B Bottom cladding piece in position

C Jig side frame components
D Wedges in position
E Base batten secured in position
F Nail holes pre-drilled through cladding

project for instruction on the need to pre-drill bolt holes and to mark side frames in pairs.

2 When these concepts have been understood, and the necessary preparation done, you will be left with marked pairs of frames which you know will accurately bolt together and accurately reflect roof pitch. Figs 6a and 6b show the relationship of side frame 'pairs'. Left and right pre-drilled frames are numbered A^1, A^2 and B^1, B^2, etc so that A^1 and A^2 are known to accurately bolt together, as are B^1 and B^2, C^1 and C^2, etc. In jig assembly B^1 will be used with A^2, B^2 will be used with C^1, C^2 with D^1, etc.

3 Place left and right frames into jig (sawn sides uppermost) and pull them securely against the base. Using a plane or circular saw remove the groove or lap from the first cladding piece, so that it will present a clean, even surface to the dovecote base or summerhouse floor on final installation. Make sure that you prepare each of the 'bottom' cladding pieces in precisely the same way, otherwise you may end up with uneven walls, some slightly higher than the others.

4 Spread a waterproof wood glue along the frames and position the first piece of cladding so that it is held firmly against the base batten and rests accurately in the jig. Secure with narrow head galvanised nails inserted through pre-drilled holes in cladding (see projects for specifications).

5 Once the first (bottom) cladding piece is secure lay all the other pieces on except the last (top) section. Ensure that all tongues are firmly in grooves etc and then nail these pieces down. When you secure the last (top) piece remember that you will need to cut out the top corner of each to accommodate the roof frames. Consequently the nail(s) used for fixing should be placed in such a way as not to interfere with this later operation.

POINTS TO WATCH
- Drive nails at the same angles as the frames lie.
- Ensure that the cladding is fitted evenly so that all panels finish to the same dimension.
- Watch out for 'rogue' cladding which has not been planed to the correct width.
- Avoid build-up of glue on the jig frames.

Jig 2. For roof section assembly (summerhouses, pergola, dovecotes)

This jig (Fig 7) should be constructed in the same way as Jig 1, but with reference to the following notes:

1 It should reflect apex angle *precisely* and the two base angles should be *identical*. Check and re-check all angles before you cut or fix anything.

2 All roof section jigs should be built so that cladding may be applied and cut in-situ. The jig frames, therefore, should not be higher than the roof section frame (Fig 7, section 1).

3 It is useful, in some circumstances, to leave a gap (Fig 7, section 2) at the apex of the jig so that a tenon saw may be used to create a flush joint at the apex of the roof frame when being assembled.

Using the roof section jig

1 Having sawn the roof frames to the appropriate angle, pre-drilled the bolt holes and numbered the timbers, you

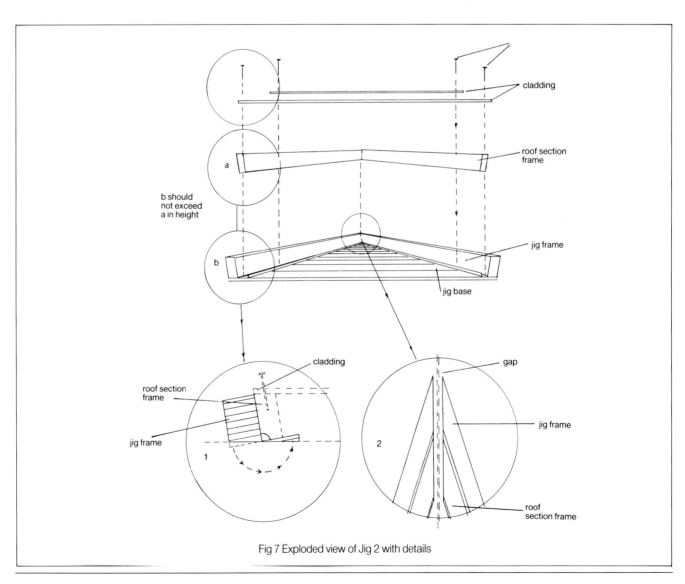

Fig 7 Exploded view of Jig 2 with details

should also cut a (35°) wedge from the end of each so that, when raised to roof pitch each will present a vertical face to the other (see pergola roof construction).

2 Lay left and right timbers in the jig (sawn side up) and, if necessary, screw them down. It is vital that they are accurately positioned. If you wish to make an absolutely flush joint at the apex use a tenon saw to further shape each frame, while it is in the jig.

3 Once you are happy that the frames are accurately positioned mark the jig so that you have a guide for later sections.

4 Begin laying on cladding, starting from the bottom (widest), spreading waterproof wood glue as you go and securing with narrow head galvanised nails. Drive these nails at the angle of the frame and be careful not to split the wood. Pre-drilling is advisable for the insertion of these nails as split wood is the last thing you want on a roof. Make certain that the cladding starts straight and continues straight. Cut each piece roughly as you go, but *do not* attempt to achieve a finish at this stage.

5 When the roof section is complete remove it from the jig and saw the ends of the cladding to the same angle as the frames using a jig-saw or circular saw, running against a batten clamped to the roof section.

6 As a way of helping to prevent the movement of water across the roof to the joints cut a shallow groove about 4in (100mm) from either edge of the roof section and along its entire length (base to apex); water meeting this channel will be directed downwards.

Windows

Simple windows for summerhouses may be constructed very easily with reference to the drawings in Fig 8. These show a plan view identifying component parts and a simple corner joint construction. Joinery grade timber should always be used, to help guard against warping and shrinkage. Joints should be screwed and glued. A tenon saw, mitre gauge and large 90° set square are essential for construction and assembly and a simple 90° jig secured to the workbench during assembly will prove very useful.

Glazing: Unless it is to be painted, ordinary white wood putty should not be used. Left unprotected it quickly dries out and begins to crack. Always use a coloured putty designed for this type of application or wooden quadrants pressed against a silicon sealant. This last option is the most satisfactory in every sense but ensure that the quadrant is properly treated before use.

Fig 8 Simple window construction
The key to the numbered section in Fig 8 is as follows:
1 Main frame timber
2 Timber nailed to main frame to form rebate and provide closure
3 Sill
4 Window frame
5 Timber nailed to window frame to provide rebate for glass
6 Glass (always use 4mm)
7 Putty or wood quadrant pressed against clear silicon

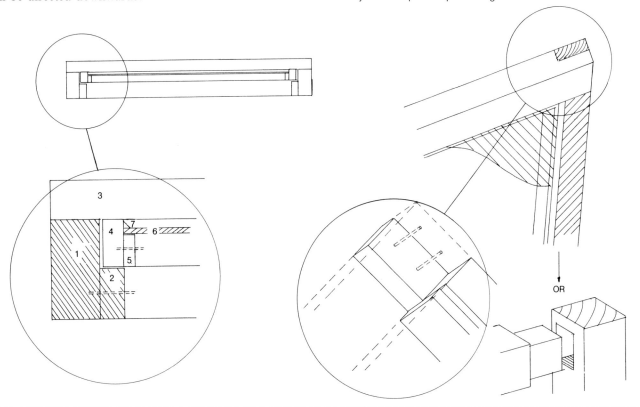

Window furniture: A wide range of window furniture is available. Brass hinges should always be used and brass catches, handles etc always look best when set against wood.

Making Tight Dowelled Mortice and Tenon Joints

It can sometimes be difficult to draw tenons very firmly into the mortice ready for a single operation dowelling; perhaps you are unable, for example, to clamp the pieces together sufficiently tightly. In many applications a great deal of strength obtains from well fitting, tight joints, and to achieve this you may wish to consider the method proposed here. Read points 1 to 5 in conjunction with the illustration.

1 Drill through until point of drill touches and marks tenon. Withdraw drill.

2 Remove tenon.

3 Continue to drill through mortice as described.

4 Place drill about ⅛in (3mm) above mark on tenon and drill through.

5 Reinstate tenon to check holes are slightly out of line. Remove. Point dowel, put glue into joint and drive dowel through with a hammer. Tenon will be pulled tightly down into mortice. Trim dowel ends. Wipe off surplus glue.

Timber

Unless otherwise specified, all the timber used in the book projects is softwood. In practice, when you order particular sections of softwood timber from the woodyard you will receive material of a type that the yard considers suitable for a particular purpose. This timber may be from any of the dozen or so types of tree which are considered to be softwood varieties. A section of 3×3in (75×75mm) post, intended for external use or as part of a carcassing structure, will probably come from a spruce or fir and is sold as whitewood, whereas planed tongue and groove timber intended for decorative cladding will be of a better quality pine most often sold as red deal. In my experience by the time timber arrives at the woodyard it has lost its particular identity and simply becomes 'softwood'. Even the staff are unlikely to be able to differentiate between the varieties in some woodyards.

There is an important botanical difference between trees classed as true softwoods (gymnosperms) and those classed as true hardwoods (angiosperms). The process that decides the softness or hardness of timber is, in general terms, the speed at which timber grows, and the nature of that growth. At one end of the scale the spruces and firs grow very rapidly with the cell manufacturing layer, the cambium, producing tissues of relatively large, weak,

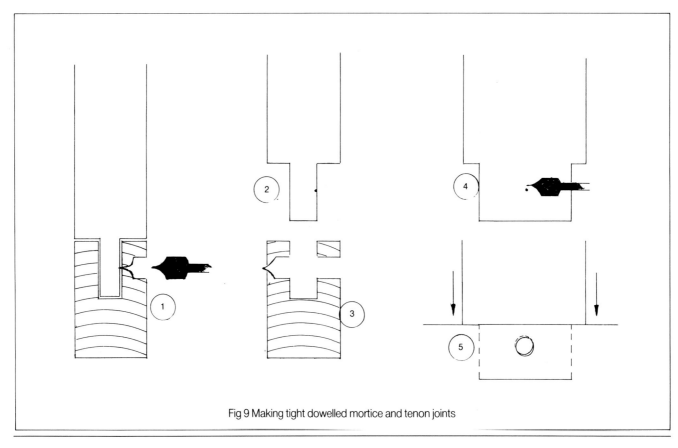

Fig 9 Making tight dowelled mortice and tenon joints

zylem cells. On the other hand oaks and other true hardwoods lay on new wood very slowly and the cells are very dense. Even within tree families there may be a considerable range of density, as that between Scots pine and pitch pine, which is actually quite a hard wood although it is classified as a softwood species.

Whereas true hardwoods such as oak are resistant to many forms of decay, their density and hardness providing a deterrent against insect attack and water penetration, softwoods do not offer much resistance to degradation. This is particularly true with new 'plantation' timbers which are selected for speed of growth and which, when sawn, still contain a high proportion of sapwood. Provided softwood timber is treated to suit its particular application its tendency to deteriorate should not present any problems, but the onus is on the user to ensure proper treatment; all woodyards will supply timber pre-treated for various applications (for Timber Treatments see below).

Another important feature of the hardness scale is the oily, or non-oily nature of the timber, and the effect this may have on paint applications. Softwoods will readily accept oil-based paint systems, but hardwoods such as teak and oak, which are naturally more oily, will tend to reject oil-based paints which will eventually peel off. The obvious conclusion is that hardwood applications around the house, such as window frames, should be stained or treated with non-oil-based products.

When selecting planed timber for use as weather boarding or for some other decorative role, be careful to reject any pieces with knots that are likely to shrink and become detached from the wood, leaving a hole. Some knotting is inevitable but it is necessary to use your judgement with each piece offered.

Timber Treatments

This section sets out to explain the nature and application of the various timber treatments and protective coatings used in the book projects. It may be that the particular systems are not available in your area, but if they are not, then there are sure to be parallel systems marketed under different names. The important thing is not what the particular treatment is called but what it does. If you intend to apply a timber treatment yourself, it is important to follow closely the instructions on the can, and the technical instructions in the leaflets which may be distributed with the product.

Tanalised timber

Tanalised timber is any suitable species of timber or type of plywood which has been impregnated with Tanalith C preservative of a specified solution strength, using an appropriate treatment cycle, and conforming to established standards. Tanalith C preservative conforms to British Standard 4072. The tanalising process proofs against degradation due to biological agencies: fungal decay, wood-destroying moulds, insect larvae, termites and marine borers. Within the accepted meaning of the word Tanalith C is permanent. It will not be washed out of wood nor lost due to volatilisation and requires no periodic re-treatment. Because of its 'fixation' properties and the fact that the component chemicals are not contact poisons, the treated and *dried* timber does not constitute a health hazard. Growing plants in contact with it are not affected, domestic animals may lick or even chew it without ill effect, and the *dry* product is safe to handle. The active ingredient is a copper arsenide compound which should not be handled while still wet, in which form it may be toxic. Tanalised timber may be recognised by its greenish hue, which provides a finish in its own right for items such as fence posts, farm buildings etc. Where a decorative appearance is required tanalised timber may be over-painted with all standard wood finishes, provided it is properly dry.

Throughout this book tanalised timber is recommended for ground contact applications (such as the supporting pole for the dovecote), and for the preparation of structural frameworks exposed to wet or damp conditions or located in situations where maintenance would be difficult (such as the base frame for the revolving summerhouse). In common with most other forms of treatment the tanalising process does not fully penetrate most sections of timber, and any treated timber which is subjected to cross-cutting or rip-sawing should have its sawn surface liberally treated with a suitable product such as Ensele or Protim to restore full protection to the wood, where that wood is likely to be in ground contact. Tanalised timbers that have been sawn but are not destined for ground contact may be treated with Sadolin (or similar).

Vacuum treatment with clear preservatives

Exterior timber (not ground contact) may also be treated against decay with clear preservatives applied by a vacuum process. This has the advantage of being fast, with timber ready for use immediately, and does not colour the wood. The process is best used for treating finished joinery components prior to final assembly, such as windows and doors. The treatment is normally in four stages: an initial vacuum reduces air pressure in the wood cells; it is then flooded with preservative at atmospheric pressure – the difference in pressure drives preservative into the wood cells. Preservative is then pumped from the vacuum chamber and a final vacuum applied. As the pressure in the chamber falls below that in the wood a substantial amount of preservative is drawn out of the wood. This empties the wood cells but leaves them coated with

SADOLIN CLASSIC (formerly PX 65). This is an organic solvent based, water repellent, decorative wood protection providing lasting protection against blue stain and moulds. It may be used for interior and exterior applications in all new softwood, hardwood, plywood etc and may also be used on previously treated timbers to give added protection or colour. It should only be used on dry timber that is clean, and oil- and dust-free. The manufacturers' instructions should be followed closely. All surfaces of the object timber must be coated to provide complete protection and this specifically includes joints or laps which may shrink or move, exposing untreated areas of timber (apply one coat of Classic to these areas before assembly). The product is supplied ready for use and should not be thinned. It should be stirred before and *during* application to ensure even distribution of pigments. It should be applied in an even, flowing coat and not 'brushed out'. Excess surface material should be re-distributed with a 'dry' brush 5–20 minutes after application, depending on absorption rate and drying conditions. Be careful not to leave drips or excess too long before finishing off, as once dry, runs and drips will be impossible to remove or mask. When re-applying Classic during normal maintenance, simply rub down the surface with a stiff brush (not a wire brush) and re-coat. The product wears through erosion.

Sadolin Classic (PX65) is used in the projects described in this book as a two-coat protective finish for light sections of timber not in contact with the ground; as a colour; and as a further protection for tanalised timber that has been sawn or planed (not in contact with the ground).

SADOLIN EXTRA (formerly Sadotop) This is an organic solvent based, high performance joinery protection with a translucent finish. It is suitable for use on all exterior and interior timbers where a degree of gloss is required, either to facilitate cleaning or to improve protection against wear. It may be used as a two-coat system in the same way as Classic, or as an additional protective coating for wood already treated with Classic. Its application and maintenance is as with Classic and the manufacturers' instructions should be closely followed.

This product is suggested for applications where a high resistance to water is required (such as the summerhouse roof); as an addition to timbers already treated with Classic; and in areas where a degree of handling is inevitable, such as windows and doors, as it offers good protection against marking and general wear.

SADOLIN SUPERDEC Superdec is a white opaque timber protection based upon a combination of alkyd and acrylic resins. It contains powerful fungicides, effective against blue stain and moulds, but is harmless to plants, animals and humans. It is vapour permeable (microporous). Superdec may be used for all exterior applications where an opaque white finish is required and is ideal for claddings, fascias etc. It is also very useful for overpainting existing stains or conventional paints where a change of colour or higher degree of durability is required. Application is by brush, as with Classic and Extra, and manufacturers' instructions should be followed closely.

Superdec is used in a number of projects which require a white finish for the purpose of design, and is used instead of conventional oil-based painting systems. It offers a high degree of whiteness and durability, as well as trouble-free maintenance when compared with the 'stripping off' of oil-based paints at the end of their useful life. It is also used as additional protection for tanalised posts that have been planed or sawn.

preservative – the surface of the timber is wet. Gradually the residual air pressure in the wood falls below atmospheric pressure. Lastly, after the vacuum pump has stopped and the recovered preservative has been pumped away, the vessel is vented to atmosphere and the difference in pressure drives the surface liquid back into the timber. This leaves the surface dry, and ready for application.

Few of the projects in this book mention this process, although it may be applicable to many of them depending on your 'finish' requirements. The process should certainly be considered for external timbers destined for oil-based painting or for sealing with oils or waxes.

Sadolin products

A number of Sadolin products are used repeatedly through the book, in a variety of applications. This just happens to be the product which I have found to be most satisfactory, but its use is not intended to imply that other, similar treatments are inferior in any way.

Graded stress timber (GS)

Timber that is used for structural, load-bearing purposes (such as floor joists and the base spans of the bridge in this book) should be graded for stress (GS), and each length of timber should carry a stamp confirming that it is suitable for use as a structural timber. The reason for this system is that all species of timber have been assessed as having characteristics making them suitable for carrying N load per N span per N thickness. Visual grading requires that a known timber of a known length is selected for its structural integrity (the grain is continuous and uninterrupted). Timber can also be machine graded (MG), which may involve the application of a test load to determine bending characteristics. Building plans subject to local authority approval may have to specify the span and section of GS timber, and its category within the range of stress grades, for its use in particular applications. The selection of the correct type and section of timber is normally with reference to a load table published by regulating bodies. For the purposes of this book it is sufficient to know that, where specified, timber should be ordered with GS of the span and section stated. This will ensure that the timber you receive has structural integrity. American and Canadian timber is subject to a similar form of assessment and stamped accordingly.

Timber sizes

When ordering from your woodyard you will generally be buying either sawn or planed timber, generally known as PSE (Planed Square Edge). The sectional size (thickness) of all timber is described in terms of the original sawn dimension of that timber. PSE timber will have lost around $\frac{3}{16}$in (5mm) in preparation so, for example, the actual size of a piece of 2×2in (50×50mm) PSE will probably be nearer to 1¾×1¾in (44×44mm). To give another example, the cladding used throughout this book is described as ¾×5in (19×125mm) but will actually measure just over ½in (13–14mm) in thickness. Tongued and grooved boards will generally be sold as 4in (100mm), 5in (125mm) etc. The actual coverage of these boards will be rather less, a 5in (125mm) board actually measuring around 4⅝in (118mm).

In the UK timber is supplied in lengths divisible by 300mm (11¹³⁄₁₆in). Metric measurement is used almost exclusively, except for some specialised or traditional items, and it is in your interest to use the metric system wherever possible. Generally you will be unable to order lengths of timber longer than 5.4m (18ft) or shorter than 2.4m (8ft). Timber should always be ordered in lengths that will suit the particular purpose and provide the minimum waste. Do not just go to the supplier with an

order for, say, 82m of cladding which you will get in a variety of lengths. Specify that the order should be in so many lengths of 3m and so many lengths of 4.2m, or whatever is required.

Fixings

Throughout this book, reference is made to the use of galvanised nails and zinc-plated screws. These rust-resistant fixings should always be used in exterior applications, particularly where their heads will show. Galvanised nails are sold by weight and there is some difference in shank and head design for particular applications. In general you will require narrow nails with small heads. In all cases nails should be inserted through pre-drilled holes to avoid damage to timber. Zinc-plated screws (or other types of rust-resistant screws) should always be used. I find the most useful type to be cross-headed screws with very open threads (fewer turns required). A Yankee screwdriver is a great help in driving these screws home.

Tools

Most of the book projects require the use of tools not normally regarded as DIY equipment. They are, however, easily available from hire shops, or you may be able to borrow from friends. One option which may be worth considering for some of the more complex projects is to have a joinery workshop prepare some of the components for you, thus obviating the need for the more specialised tool. Below is a brief description of some of the tools you may need, and some hints on their safe and effective use.

Circular saw

A hand-held circular saw is required in many projects and should have the following features:

- Adjustable pitch of blade (to 45°).
- Adjustable guide.
- Protected blade.
- Tungsten tipped blade (if possible).
- 7in (18cm) blade (minimum).
- Adjustable cutting depth (to 2½in (6cm) ideally).

When setting the saw for a particular cut check the result on a piece of waste timber before committing yourself to the object wood. Always ensure that the footplate of the saw is flush onto the surface during cutting. Wherever possible use a piece of timber to guide the saw footplate. This is generally more accurate, and faster, than using the saw guide. When cutting through large sections of timber it is often advisable to make two or three passes through the wood, at increasing depths. This will place

---

Some tips on how to deal with timber buying.

Delivery: If you are buying long lengths of timber always ask for it to be delivered. It will probably cost nothing, provided you live within normal delivery range, and will usually be very quick. Unless you have a large estate car with a ladder rack you will probably have difficulty in handling useful lengths of timber anyway.

Condition: When buying quantities of timber there will often be the odd damaged length. Although you can, of course, return this to the woodyard, it is often worthwhile (when you can realistically still use the timber efficiently) to tell them that it was damaged and ask for a price reduction for that length. They are unlikely to want that length back and should be very happy for you to keep it at a reduced price.

Knots: Watch out for excessively knotty wood, particularly when that wood is destined for an exposed environment, such as a summerhouse roof. Knots have a tendency to shrink and fall out and you could do without that on a roof or wall.

Straightness: In my experience there is no such thing as a straight piece of softwood. You can get somewhere close to it if you pick your way through the shelves, but do not expect miracles and never assume that the wood you are using to make a critical template is true. Most sections of softwood can be brought into true during assembly.

Special treatments: Order any treated timbers well in advance because, if the particular section you require is not held in stock, there may be a considerable delay in having the treatment carried out and the timber dried. Allow around two weeks for special treatments.

Price: If you are buying a large quantity of timber (as you will be in some of the book projects) you should ask for a discount, if one is not automatically offered. It will certainly be worth your while phoning round and getting quotes from a variety of sources before committing yourself to one supply. Always buy from a builders' timber yard, rather than a corner shop or DIY store. Corner shops will always be expensive because they will be buying their stock from the builders' yard, and DIY homecentres, even though they may say their goods are cheap, may not be when compared with the builders.

less stress on the motor and should leave you with a cleaner cut. In common with jig-saws the cutting action of circular saws is *upwards* through the wood. This means that the side facing upwards will be more ragged than the downwards-facing side. When cutting timber whose face will show in final assembly this point should be born in mind. Experiment with a piece of timber to fully understand this point.

SAFETY NOTE

Many regard the hand-held circular saw as a dangerous tool, and its safe use cannot be stressed too greatly. Before using the saw make sure that you fully understand the way that it works, and in particular the position of the blade in relation to your fingers, the direction of the blade's travel and the placement of the power cable in relation to object wood.

Always wear safety glasses when using the saw and make sure that the blade is sharp.

Electric plane

A hand-held electric plane is useful for many projects and should display the following features:

- Two-handed grip.
- Planing depth adjustable to $\frac{1}{16}$in (1.5mm).
- Reversible and changeable blades.
- Collection bag.

Always use the plane in long strokes, being careful not to dig the blade in at the beginning of each stroke. If planing across end grain do not allow the blade to 'exit' from the timber. Always plane *in* to the timber, first from one side, then from the other. In this way you will avoid tearing the wood. It is worth experimenting with this, and the use of the plane generally, before committing yourself to the real thing. If used *very carefully* particularly with regard to planing across the grain, an electric plane can be a great labour-saver in the preparation of tenon joints, once the dimension of the joint has been defined with a tenon saw. When using an electric plane on surfaces wider than the plane always use a shallow setting and be very sure to keep the plane level. Plane the whole width of timber with equal strokes before starting at the beginning again. This even planing will help to avoid gouge marks along the grain that over-ambitious planing may cause.

Jig saw

A hand-held jig-saw, of any type, will also be useful in many projects. The choice of blade is rather more important than the choice of saw, particularly if you need to produce shapes or scrolls. As with the circular saw the cutting action of the jig-saw is upwards. This will tend to leave a ragged edge on the upwards-facing surface which should be taken into account when preparing timber that will 'show'. Some jig-saws come with a gadget that reduces part of the tearing action of the saw.

Router

A plunge router, although not required in the projects, is nevertheless a very useful tool, particularly for the embellishment of fascia timber or in cutting shapes. Be careful not to overload the machine with too large a cutting bit or in trying to cut too deep in one stroke. My router responds to the vibrations caused by this form of overloading by breaking wires inside the relays and this is a complication that you could do without. Before using a router be sure to read the handbook or other instructions carefully – there are right ways and wrong ways, particularly in the direction of work.

Other tools

Apart from the specialised tools mentioned above you should need only an ordinary selection of hand tools and instruments. These are listed below for your interest. The list should be regarded as a minimum requirement for all projects and does not include items such as box forms for cutting angles, which you may already have and which could be quite useful.

An *electric drill*, with a full range of bits, including $\frac{1}{2}$in and 1in (13 and 25mm) flat wood bits is essential. In my workshop I use a mains-powered drill alongside a 'cordless' drill, equipped with a screwdriver bit – this combination speeds up work enormously in certain processes. Cordless drills are ideal for most applications up to $\frac{1}{4}$in (6mm) bits. They are not suitable for masonry drilling or drilling with flat wood bits so are only really useful in conjunction with a mains drill.

A good quality *Yankee screwdriver* (*ie* a screwdriver with a sprung push action) with a choice of bits is invaluable in the time and energy it saves, even in the most routine jobs like doorhanging.

Mallet
Chisels – a good range of chisels and an oil stone (with suitable oil)
Claw hammer
Combination square
Spirit level
Mortice gauge
Tenon saw
Cross-cut saw
Bradawl
Tape measure
Two 'G'-clamps (6in (15cm))
Stanley knife
Sandpaper (plus drill attached sanding pad ideally)

360° protractor
30°/60° set square
Screwdrivers
Adjustable spanner
Sliding bevel

Large-scale woodworking machinery
The projects in this book are directed very much at the ordinary DIY person with limited access to saw-benches, planing machines etc. Those hobbyists and small professionals who wish to use the projects and have access to larger machinery will find the use of a circular saw bench, with angle facility, a great time-saver. It is my experience, however, that for the more complicated projects such as the dovecote, unless you are actually making a production run, the time spent building guides for band-saws etc is not worthwhile. Better to stick with the known quantities of the templates and jigs outlined in the book. The chances are that the small professional will have his own ideas about many of the projects outlined and will adapt the design and production accordingly.

4 Projects

1 Arboured Path

A pergola may be used to great effect in the creation of an arboured pathway, with shade and interest being provided by climbing plants such as clematis and rose, growing up and across the slatted structure. Purpose-built structures such as this are particularly useful in more formal gardens with long, straight walks where the design can be used to 'connect' different parts of the garden, as well as to give interest to large, possibly monotonous areas of lawn. In my own garden most of the potential south-facing beds are cast into shade by large trees which, because of their size and the spread of their branches, are unsuitable as hosts for all but the largest clematis. In many gardens an arboured path could provide additional south-facing growing areas, bringing plants out from the shade to play a leading role in garden design.

Detail showing finished assembly with secondary wire grid in place

The illustrated project is intended to be a 'dainty', unobtrusive structure whose colour and style fit in with the small, neat garden in which it stands. Some arboured paths rely on enormous sections of timber spanning brick pillars, some are made in the 'rustic' style, of branches joined together with 4in (100mm) nails; neither of these types owes much to any sense of design.

The sections of timber used in this project are suitable for a pergola with a span between posts (along the path) of up to 10ft (3m) and a width of up to 6ft 6in (2m); you will need to upgrade timbers for longer or wider spans. Lengths of timber are not specified, as it is assumed that requirements will vary for particular applications.

MATERIALS

Posts: Lengths of 3×3in (75×75mm) tanalised timber.
Frames: 4×1in (100×25mm) PSE softwood.
Slats: 1×1½in (25×38mm) PSE softwood batten.
Brackets: 1×1½in (25×38mm) PSE softwood batten.
Secondary grid: Plastic-coated wire.
Fixings: 2in (50mm) no 8 zinc-plated screws. 2in (50mm) galvanised nails.

SPECIAL TOOLS

Electric plane for preparing 'sawn' post timbers.
Fret-saw or jig-saw for decorative work.

Construction

Before buying any materials consider carefully the main points of design:

1 Overall length of structure. The pergola should look as though it is meant to be there, which usually means that it connects one part of the garden with another. A structure in the middle of the lawn which nobody would have a good reason to walk through might look a bit odd.

2 Spacing and height of posts. A structure some distance from the normal viewpoint may need to be taller and broader than usual to bring it into play as a significant design feature for the overall garden. A pergola built with a screening role in mind should be more 'closed', with narrower spans between posts than one crossing the line of sight down a garden.

3 Width of path. Be sure to make the path wide enough to walk down without constantly being attacked by roses or other plants growing into the path area.

The construction is intended to be entirely flexible and, with a little planning, you should be able to introduce bends and other interesting features into the design.

Posts

Prepare lengths of 3×3in (75×75mm) tanalised post (ground-contact timber must be tanalised, or similarly treated – see Timber Treatments p.55). Allow 24in (600mm) for insertion below ground level. Using an electric plane smooth the posts and slightly chamfer the corners to disguise their 'squareness' (*do not* plane or chamfer the end of post destined for the ground, or the effectiveness of the timber treatment will be compromised).

Fig 1 Cross joint for spanning timber

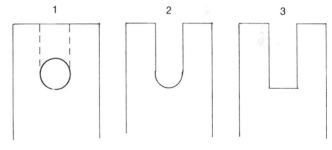

Fig 2 Cross joint preparation

Using a tenon saw and sharp chisel cut cross joints from the end of each post (Figs 1 and 4). These joints are to receive the spanning timbers running along and across the structure, and should be marked out and cut to suit. The preparation of these joints may be hastened by drilling out the bottom of each slot (1), sawing down to it (2), and finally trimming the bottom square with a chisel (3). The (four) posts at each end of the structure should only be jointed to receive one cross timber and one 'length' timber; they should be jointed with a T, so that the ends remain flush.

Spanning Timber

Prepare lengths of 4×1in (100×25mm) PSE softwood to span across the path, and test each one in the appropriate post joints (Fig 3). Allow a reasonable overlap beyond each post and measure for a decorative finish at the end of each spanning timber. Cut the pattern from a piece of ply or hardboard and use this as an accurate template for marking each of the timbers. Use a jig-saw or fret-saw to prepare timber and thoroughly sand edges. Fig 3 shows this procedure.

Prepare further lengths of timber, with precisely square ends, to span 'along' the pergola between posts. In final assembly these timbers will abut the cross frames as they are inserted into the post joints (Fig 5; also Fig 1).

Fig 3 Preparing spanning timber

Fig 4 Using a spirit level during positioning of supporting posts and spanning timbers

Fig 5 Post joint showing timbers in position

Installation of Posts and Frames

With all posts and main frame timbers complete, measure out and mark the ground for post positions. Dig pairs of post holes 24in (600mm) deep and 18in (450mm) square to receive posts loosely connected by a spanning timber. Correctly space and level posts and spanning timber before compacting soil around posts (in particularly weak ground or very exposed positions, it may be advisable to pour a concrete foundation). Complete one pair of posts before progressing to the next, using spanning timbers to establish precise post positions and levels. Insert spanning timbers as you go but *do not* secure at this stage (unless all timbers have already been painted).

Once all posts are in position, and you know that spanning timbers fit precisely, remove these timbers and paint both posts and timbers with a water-repellent preservative treatment such as Sadolin. The illustrated project has been painted with opaque white Sadolin Pinotex Superdec (posts) and walnut Sadolin Classic (PX65) (framework and slats), applied in accordance with the manufacturers' instructions.

With all timbers treated and dried, reassemble the framework as in Fig 4 and secure timbers using 2in (50mm) no 8 zinc-plated screws. Most of these screws can be inserted very discreetly, with 'lengths' of timber being secured with screws inserted through 'spanning' timbers into end grain.

Slats

With the framework completed, prepare and paint lengths of 1×1½in (25×38mm) softwood slat. Secure each slat with one 2in (50mm) galvanised nail inserted through a pre-drilled hole into the frame timber. Slats should be laid narrow-side down. The slats in the illustrated project are spaced 12in (300mm) apart. Fig 6 shows them being secured.

You may choose to reduce the grid size (to make things easier for climbing plants) by installing a secondary grid of plastic coated wire as shown on p.64. This wire will be hardly discernible to the eye but will provide ideal support for plants. Pre-drill each slat to accept this wire *before* installation, using a single drilled slat as a pattern for the rest.

Fig 6 Securing slats across framework

Brackets

With all slats completed prepare lengths of batten to provide 45° brackets between posts and frames. Although these brackets will provide some additional support and rigidity to the structure their main role is to create a visually pleasing link between posts and frames. Without this device the pergola would tend to look very square.

TRAINING PLANTS
Young plants may need to be assisted up the posts with wire trellis or similar. Once plants are established these supports may be removed.

---

2 Trellis

There is nothing so potentially effective as trelliswork for climbing plants; even the plainest wall can be transformed by a wisteria or clematis climbing up and through a good trellis.

Wisteria is an attractive and popular climbing plant

What makes a *good* trellis? Too often a trellis is seen merely as the means by which plants may be trained up a wall, rather than as a feature in its own right. This leads to a careless choice of design and colour and, as often as not, the purchase of lengths of ready-made expanding trellis that does not fit, in either the practical or the aesthetic sense. The measure of a *good* trellis should be that it is an attractive addition to the wall, or other supporting structure, even before plants are added. To achieve this the following points should be appreciated:

- The timber being used must be substantial enough to 'look as though it should be there'. Good quality planed and treated softwood should always be used – an ideal section is ¾×1½in (19×38mm).
- The trellis should be held away from the wall far enough to cast shadows, which will add interest and perspective to the structure. A 'thin' trellis held close to the wall will look two dimensional.
- The grid system must be in keeping with the bearing structure. A house will respond better to a structure that reflects its design, and this will normally be best achieved with a square or rectangular pattern – diagonal trellis will often look like an afterthought on a formal wall, although it certainly has a place in the garden.
- Does the trellis fit? It should always be tailored to fit round windows and doors so that trellis and overall architecture complement each other. Careful shaping will help to make the trellis look as though it *belongs*.
- Does the colour of the trellis suit its bearing wall? Can colour be used to contrast with the bearing wall and improve the overall design of wall or house? The most suitable colour for a trellis is often white, particularly when seen against the greens of foliage and the range of brick colours and textures. Modern opaque white-wood treatments take all the heartache out of the white painting associated with conventional oil-based systems.
- Is the trellis large enough? There seems little point in building a 6ft (1.8m) trellis against an 18ft (5m) wall, where the structure will probably be 'lost' from any meaningful influence on design. Indeed, little bits of low trellis dotted around a building can often detract from overall design.

The construction of any trellis is a very simple matter, success owing rather more to correct measurement and the use of appropriate materials and colour than to particular construction techniques. There are, however, some further points to consider before starting construction.

What plants are intended for the trellis? What is the nature of their growth and required pruning? A clematis *montana*, for example, requires no pruning and may very quickly grow to 20ft (6m) or more, whereas clematis *jackmanii* requires heavy pruning and is unlikely to grow more than 10ft (3m) in a season. This means that the *montana* will not need much support for its lower structure after the first year, while *jackmanii* will always need something to climb up. This sort of characteristic will help you to decide at what level the trellis should start, and to what height it should be built. It is just as important to consider how much your climbing plants will spread. Wisteria, for example, will tend to produce rather more lateral growth than vertical, so a wisteria trellis should always provide plenty of scope for this sideways growth.

Most gardening books suggest a grid size of 9in (225mm) for climbing plants. I see no reason to abide by this rather limiting dimension; it is surely more important to construct a grid system sympathetic to the bearing structure and then, if necessary, add a discreet secondary grid of plastic-coated wire. This is demonstrated in Fig 1. The grid size in the illustrated project is 12×24in (300× 600mm), which is probably the most suitable for the plants grown on it, and the bearing structure.

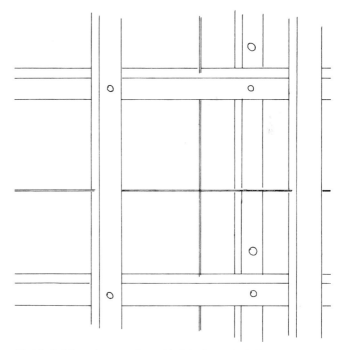

Fig 1 Installation of a secondary grid of plastic-coated wire

---

MATERIALS

(Structural) Trellis: ¾ × 1½in (19 × 38mm) tanalised planed batten
(Garden) Trellis: ½ × 1½in (12 × 38mm) tanalised planed batten
Fixings: Zinc-plated screws 1¼in (31mm) no 8 (or smaller for garden trellis).
Colour/treatment: Opaque white microporous wood treatment such as Sadolin Superdec. Coloured wood treatments such as Sadolin Classic or other spirit-based preservative treatments.

Construction

With regard to the particular requirements of the site, decide on the height and width of trellis and, if possible, work out how you may prefabricate sections of the structure, for joining together in-situ. The illustrated trellis, for example, was made in three sections (spans between windows, and windows and door) joined together with spars running above the windows.

On a level surface lay out the vertical slats, cut to required lengths with a tenon saw, and use a combination square to mark across these the positions for horizontal slats.

Position the slats at required spacings and lay on horizontal slats, cut to length, one at a time. Pre-drill at each cross-over point for the insertion of 1¼in (31mm) no 8 zinc-plated screws.

Paint each completed section with opaque white-wood treatment or coloured preservative, applied according to the manufacturers' instructions. Pay particular attention to the painting of end-grain exposed through sawing.

As in Fig 1, secure lengths of painted batten to the wall with zinc-plated screws driven into plugged holes in the masonry. These battens will serve to keep the trellis away from the wall, providing room for the plants to run behind the trellis and giving 'depth' to the structure. Insert supporting battens at top and bottom of the structure and, for very large areas, at 6ft (1.8m) spacings. Secure trellis sections to the wall-mounted battens with zinc-plated screws.

If necessary, position plastic-coated wire to reduce grid size. This may be purchased in long lengths and should be fed through pre-drilled holes in the trellis to achieve the required grid size. The aim should be to create a discreet climbing frame that meets the particular requirements of plants without compromising the main trellis design.

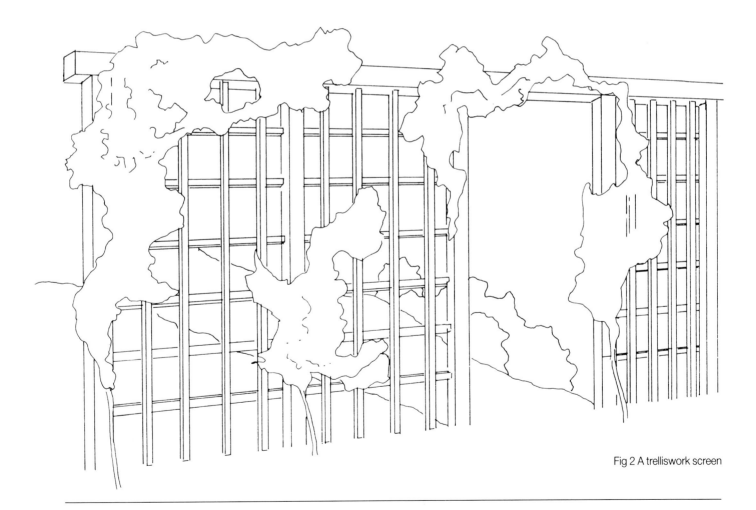

Fig 2 A trelliswork screen

Diagonal Trellis

Fig 3 shows the simple construction of a diagonal trellis laid onto a wall-mounted batten. Precisely the same rules apply to this type of trellis as to the illustrated project.

Trelliswork Screen

Fig 2 shows a design for a trellis screen, used to train plants and create an interesting perspective along a pathway, or to obscure an unsightly view. This is certainly one of the most effective applications for trellis, particularly in south-facing positions where the plants will flower towards the house or viewpoint.

Posts for the screen should be tanalised softwood of 3×3in (75×75mm) or 4×4in (100×100mm) section, crossed by timber of similar or slightly larger dimension, and secured with long galvanised nails. Ideally each post should be inserted into a 24in (600mm) hole and secured with 9in (225mm) of concrete (6 parts ballast to 1 part cement). The framework should be constructed as already described and be of a grid size to suit the particular purpose – if the role of the screen is to obscure, then grid size should be small; if it is to be of more open design so as to look 'through' the structure to the garden beyond, then grid size should be large, possibly supplemented with a wire grid as previously described.

The trellis screen should be fixed to the supporting structure by screwing lateral trellis pieces to an additional trellis batten secured to the inside of upright posts.

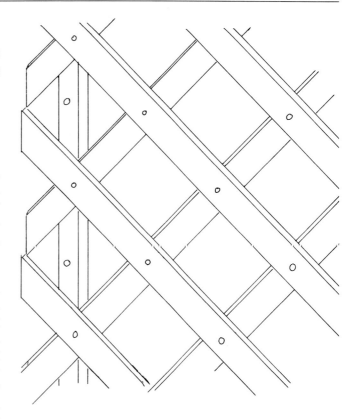

Fig 3 Diagonal trellis

3 Footbridge

It is almost worth making a water garden or in some way diverting a stream through the garden just to have a bridge. It is almost impossible to walk over one without stopping to lean over to see what is going on – there is a fascination about water, and the different world it holds, that is irresistible. While the view from the bridge is usually worthwhile, the character and style of the structure itself is sometimes rather less interesting. It can be fairly basic, for example just a couple of telegraph poles across a stream, spanned with planks. Whilst admirably serving a purpose, aesthetically this sort of design leaves something to be desired. Using modern preservative treatments and load-spreading construction techniques, enormous sections of timber are no longer required, even for quite long spans, and this serves to bring the cost of a very attractive bridge that will last for decades, to within very acceptable levels.

Checking that the spanning timbers are level

The bridge illustrated on p.79 is in part of a garden not generally accessible to young children. It is also gated. From a safety point of view, if your bridge is to be available to young, unsupervised children, then you may consider it wise to reduce the spacings of the infill cross-pieces. This may be done by adding additional diagonals; by changing to a square latticework; or by upright sections.

The bridge illustrated in this chapter spans just over 13ft (4m) and is suitable for crossing about 10ft (3m) of open water, having allowed for securing posts in either bank. If this span is not appropriate for your particular purpose, you should adjust your timber order accordingly (having read and understood the construction methods).

Without changing the specification of capital timbers (base spans and handrails) you will be able to span 20ft (6m). Be sure to order GS (grade stressed) timber for the load-bearing spans. As the name suggests this is timber that has been inspected to identify any weaknesses in structure. It may be recognised by a dye stamp stating that it is GS and specifying the length and British standard number.

For spans beyond 20ft (6m) you should seek the advice of an engineer to ascertain the section and type of timber required for a given load. For long spans an ideal material to use is 'Glu lam', which, as the name implies, is a composite of lengths of timber glued and laminated together. Its normal building use is in load-bearing structural roles where a steel joist would be an eyesore.

The bridge illustrated is designed to go from one raised bank to another. In a situation where banks are more or less flush with the water, or a higher clearance is required, say for the passage of boats, I would suggest that the same design could be used but with much longer and stouter end posts and a series of steps leading up to, and down from, the main bridge platform. Although raised, curved bridges are very attractive, they can also be disastrous for children and old people in wet or icy conditions.

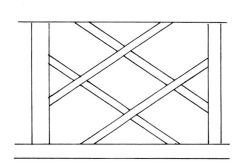

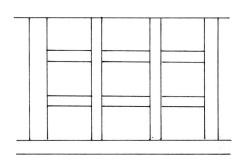

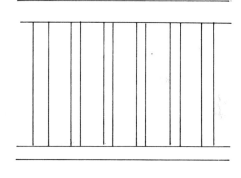

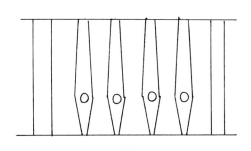

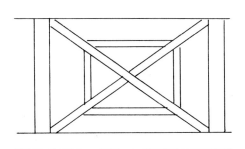

Fig 1 Various designs for the bridge sides

<hr />

MATERIALS
Footbridge with 13ft (4m) span and 46in (1.15m) width

3×3in (75×75mm) tanalised sawn softwood post
    Four, in 6ft (1.8m) lengths (end posts)
    Two at 39in (1m) (uprights for gate)
7×2in (175×50mm) tanalised GS (grade-stressed) sawn softwood
    Two at 14ft (4.2m) (base rails)
4×2in (100×50mm) tanalised sawn softwood
    Two at 14ft (4.2m) (handrails)
    Two at 10ft (3m) (uprights, six at 39in (1m))
    Two at 39in (1m) (rails for gate)
1½×1½in (38×38mm) PSE (planed square edge)
    80ft (24m) in long lengths (infill)
7×1½in (175×38mm) tanalised sawn plank to cut twenty at 46in
    (1.15m) lengths plus six at 1ft (300mm) lengths (walkway)
8ft (1.8m) × ½in (12mm) hardwood dowel
Fixings: Thirty-six 1½in (38mm) no 8 zinc screws (cross head)
Nine 1¼in (31mm) no 8 zinc screws (cross head)
1lb (½ kilo) 3in (75mm) galvanised nails
Gate hinges, screws and latch
1 bag of cement and quantity of ballast
Heavy wire or scrap metal to reinforce concrete
Small quantity of hardcore
Colour/Treatment: Wood treatment/stain (Sadolin Classic)

SPECIAL TOOLS
Electric plane
1in (25mm) flat wood bit
Circular saw (not essential but may save time in cutting timber to length)

Construction

The principle of construction for this bridge is the workshop preparation of two complete sides which may be installed into concrete foundations and then spanned with a timber walkway. Each side is a cohesive and very strong arrangement of jointed timbers, with loads spread through the structure. Tanalised timber is used for all capital timbers, and this ensures maintenance-free longevity, which is particularly important in the damp atmosphere likely to prevail at the intended site.

The Sides

Before starting construction, plane and slightly chamfer all 'sawn' timber with the exception of the floor planks (which *should* be left in their rough state) and the inside faces of base spans (which will not be seen).

As in Fig 2, clamp together a length of 7×2in (175×50mm) (for the base rail), and an equivalent length of 4×2in (100×50mm) (for the handrail), so that the surfaces are flush and ends parallel. Decide which side of the bridge you are making and turn the unplaned face of base timber accordingly.

Using a combination square, mark for 2in (50mm) tenons at each end of the timbers and measure the distance between these marks. On each timber, divide this distance into four equal spans and mark the three post positions – using a square, draw lines through these positions; on each side of these three lines, draw further lines at precisely ⅜in (9.5mm) and 1¼in (31mm). Bisect these lines with a further line drawn exactly centrally lengthways along the timbers. The points where this lengthways line crosses the ⅜in (9.5mm) and the 1¼in (31mm) lines defines the drilling positions for preparing each mortice joint (Fig 2). Make an impression at each of these points with a bradawl or nail and, using a 1in (25mm) flat wood bit, drill out each mortice joint 2in (50mm) deep and finish with a sharp chisel. Leave the ends rounded (Fig 2). Preparing mortices of this dimension will allow a ¼in (6mm) shoulder at either end of the matching tenon.

Fig 2 Preparing mortice joints in handrails and base rails

When you have prepared all six mortices separate the timbers and prepare tenons 1in (25mm) thick and 2in (50mm) deep in each end. To do this, continue the pencil lines you have already made completely around the timbers and saw through the broad sides up to these marks and to the required depth.

Remove waste wood from the tenons with a broad chisel and provide each tenon with a ¼in (6mm) shoulder, rounded to match the mortices you will be making in the posts later (refer to those already completed).

Prepare three 39in (1m) lengths of 4×2in (100×50mm) tanalised timber (for uprights) and cut tenons 1in (25mm) thick by 2in (50mm) deep in each end (six tenons). Test these tenons in the mortices already prepared (Fig 3) and ensure that the shoulders abut properly. Make any necessary adjustments and then glue each tenon into its mortice with waterproof wood glue, firmly driving each tenon home.

Fig 3 Testing mortice and tenon joints prior to assembly

Dowelling

Holes for dowelling should be drilled before gluing up, *ie* whilst the joint is dry. To obtain a really tight fit, that will pull the tenon down into the mortice, the hole through the tenon should be just out of line with the holes in the mortice sides. An explanation of this technique may be found on p.54.

Cut six 3in (75mm) lengths of dowel and round one end of each (this facilitates entry and reduces the risk of damage to wood on exit). Drill through joints you have prepared (1in (25mm) from edge) with a ½in (12.5mm) flat wood bit. Do not allow the bit to 'exit' from the wood. As soon as the leading point of the drill bit breaks surface, withdraw the bit and finish the hole from the 'wrong' side. This will prevent damage to the area around the hole, which may be caused by flat bits.

Run a small amount of waterproof wood glue into each hole before driving in the dowels, round end first. Trim off surplus with a saw or chisel and sand down rough edges. Fig 4 illustrates a dowel joint.

Fig 4 Inserting dowel peg through mortice and tenon joint

End Posts

Take two 6ft (1.8m) lengths of 3×3in (75×75mm) tanalised posts and mark positions for mortices to receive the tenons already prepared in spanning timbers. Fig 5 shows the approximate relationship of posts to spanning timbers *ie* with 3–4in (75–100mm) protruding above the handrail. Prepare these joints as already described and finally secure the assembly with one dowel per handrail and two dowels per base rail. (Before final fixing you may be wise to check that the structure will move out of the workshop in one piece. If this is not possible you should assemble the components at the bridge site.)

Fig 5 Checking that the spanning timbers are level

Cross Timbers

With the completed side assembly laid on the bench or some other level surface prepare lengths of $1\frac{1}{2}\times1\frac{1}{2}$in ($38\times38$mm) PSE, to fit as can be seen in the illustration on p.72. The two timbers required for each section should cross with a 45° simple half-lap joint, glued and secured with a single $1\frac{1}{4}$in (31mm) no 8 zinc screw. The timbers should joint into each corner in such a way that a $1\frac{1}{2}$in (38mm) no 8 zinc screw may be inserted into the uprights (through pre-drilled holes). Ensure that each timber is accurately positioned by laying on and marking each span individually.

You may choose to paint these cross timbers white, or some other shade, to contrast with the main structure. If so, remove for painting and reinstate at a later stage. An ideal product for white painting is Sadolin Pinotex Superdec, a white opaque microporous wood treatment that will not crack or blister as oil-based systems tend to.

When one side of the bridge is complete, repeat the process for the second side and then begin to build the gate, if one is required.

The Gate

Using the jointing techniques already experienced and described, build a gate (Fig 6) using two 39in (1m) lengths of 3×3in (75×75mm) tanalised post as uprights, and 4×2in (100×50mm) timber as rails. The finished gate should span 39in (1m).

Installation

This bridge will derive much of its lateral strength and stability from a substantial concrete strip foundation connecting the base of each post. The suggested construction of these foundation strips is shown in Fig 7 and it

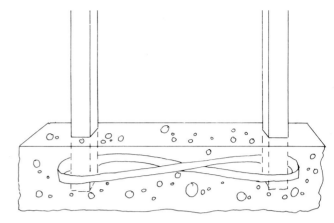

Fig 7 Showing bridge posts which sit in concrete strip foundation with metal reinforcement

is worthwhile making a really good job of it. As well as connecting and strengthening the bridge structure the foundations will serve to spread the bridge load through what may be a very weak soil structure, so close to running water.

After measuring to establish post positions, dig trenches of sufficient depth to accept posts and line these with hardcore, compacted to form a firm base. Support each post in its intended position while pouring in at least 8in (200mm) of concrete. A mix of 5 or 6 parts ballast to 1 part ordinary Portland cement is ideal. Before pouring the concrete, wrap heavy wire round the base of each post and between the two posts to reinforce the concrete. Push other scrap metal into the concrete during pouring. Check all levels as you go along and be particularly careful to keep one side of the bridge level with the other along its length. Ensure the correct spacing between sides by holding the gate in place, allowing some room for opening and closing. Tie the sides together temporarily with lengths of timber (Fig 8) while fixing the concrete.

When concrete is set (24 hours), trim walkway planks to

Fig 6 Construction of the gate

Fig 8 Checking spacing and level between sides

sit precisely onto base rails. Allow a small gap (say ½in (12mm)) between boards and fix with two 3in (75mm) galvanised nails at either end, driven into the base rail. When assessing the gap between the boards take an overall measurement and work out spacings accordingly. You will be unable to lay the planks directly onto base rails where uprights joint into the base rails. At these points nail 12in (300mm) lengths of 7×1½in (175×38mm) plank on the inside of the base rails. Use these to support planks. Fig 7 illustrates the completed walkway.

Hang the gate on strong, rustproof (galvanised or painted) hinges and fix with zinc screws.

Wood Treatment, Finishing Off

When the structure is complete, treat and stain all timber with a product such as Sadolin Classic (PX 65) in a colour of your choice.

Build up the banks or lay paving to connect with the walkway as required.

Fig 9 Wood treatment

4 Wildfowl nesting box

This project is offered as an attractive design which will enhance any pond. Serious wildfowl breeders may criticise the size of the nest area and entrance, both of which are perhaps too large for the occupant to defend properly against jackdaws or other egg thieves. My defence would be that the nesting box is designed primarily as an unusual and attractive item of garden furniture, and that despite criticism, as a wildfowl nesting box it stands a very reasonable chance of attracting a breeding pair, offering them a safe and comfortable area to raise their young.

The obvious advantage of the design is that it is safe from land predators such as cats, dogs, foxes and rats. The knowledgeable individual will adapt the design for specialist breeding purposes, and changes would have to be made if, for example, the box is intended for smaller fowl such as teal, widgeon or mandarin.

(*opposite*) Footbridge (Project 3)

The nest box illustrated is placed in a moat, the water level of which rises and falls about 10in (250mm) during the year. This degree of change may be accommodated in the design with the provision of a long ramp. With waters subject to rather greater variation you may consider placing the nest box on a floating platform, held in place with a weighted nylon rope or chain.

Another question which should be considered before you decide on any particular method of installation, is whether you will be able to drive a post into the bed of your pond. Although you may think that the bottom is nice and soft, it may not be, and you could end up, as I have done, trying to bash a post into solid ground with a 14lb hammer – while standing in a dinghy.

This project, more than any other in the book, requires the use of treated timbers and rust-proof fixings. It is also the perfect subject for modern microporous wood treatments – if the opaque white wood treatment is used, the 'whiteness' of the structure provides a clear mirror image in the water which enhances the view considerably.

The materials list and specifications are for production of a nesting box with a base 39in (1m) × 19½in (500mm) and nest-box entrance 7×10in (175×250mm). It is left to the reader to scale these dimensions down to suit particular birds.

MATERIALS

Base: 16ft 3in (5m) of 5×1in (125×25mm) (preferably) tanalised tongue and groove floorboard

Side cladding: 27ft 6in (11m) of 5×¾in (125×19mm) tongue and groove 'V' or 'matching' softwood

Roof cladding: 26ft (8m) of 5×¾in (125×19mm) shiplap

Frames: 26ft (8m) of 1×1½in (25×38mm) softwood batten
39in (1m) of ½×1½in (12×38mm) softwood batten
39in (1m) of hardwood moulding (birdsmouth)

Post: Length of 3×3in (75×75mm) tanalised post

Brackets: 5ft (1.5m) 2×2in (50×50mm) tanalised (sawn) softwood

Ramp: Tanalised 4×1in (100×25mm) plank and slats of appropriate length

Fixings: 1¼ and 1½in (31–38mm) small head galvanised nails
1¼ and 1½in (31–38mm) no 8 zinc-plated screws
6×2½in (63mm) no 10/12 zinc-plated screws

TOOLS

No special tools are required for this project although you may need a fret-saw, jig-saw or router to cut out the nest-box entrance.

Construction

Base Take five 39in (1m) lengths of 5×1in (125×25mm) tongue and groove floorboard, and fit together to define an accurate rectangular shape. Cut two 20in (500mm) lengths of 1×1½in (25×38mm) batten to fit across the base, and glue and screw these as in Fig 1 (glue along length and insert single screws towards the end of each piece). This is to locate battens for final fixing with galvanised nails. With battens in place, turn base over and nail through base into battens using 1½in (38mm) galvanised nails, inserted through pre-drilled holes. With battens secured, remove surplus timber from either side to define the finished base, 39in (1m) × 19½in (500mm). Plane or sand all edges.

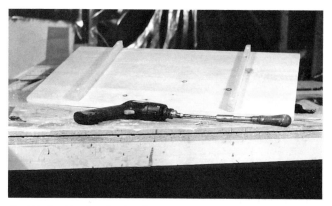

Fig 1 Underside of nesting box base

Unless you are using tanalised or vacuum-treated timber, thoroughly treat the base with a clear preservative at this stage (see Chapter 3 p.55 for advice on wood treatments and their application).

As in Fig 2, secure a framework of battens flush to the base to define the nest-box area. To assist in the measurement for this framework cut a length of tongue and groove cladding 28in (700mm) long. This will be the (absolute) length of each side, and using this and a shorter

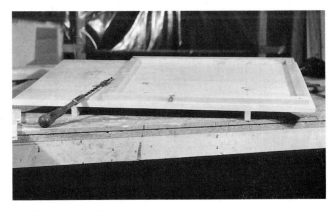

Fig 2 Framework defining nest box area

---

piece of cladding to assess the width, you can define the lengths of batten required for the frame and their exact position. Fit battens so that the finished sides and back will overhang the edge of the base and shed water *away* from it (see p.80). Glue and screw battens with 1¼ or 1½in (31–38mm) no 8 zinc-plated screws.

You should now have a finished base and know that the side, front and back cladding will fit properly against each other and against the framework.

Sides/roof (Note: for side and roof frames use 1×1½in (25×38mm) batten.) Prepare four 15in (375mm) lengths of batten and form a 35° angle in one end of each. These will provide seats for roof frames (Fig 3). Prepare eight 28in (700mm) lengths of cladding (four each side) and glue and nail to the prepared battens to produce two sides to fit precisely against the base frame – see Fig 3); the leading edge of the side cladding must extend (by its own thickness) beyond the vertical framework so as to provide a neat join with cladding pieces for front and back. With the two sides prepared, but not installed, trim the top cladding pieces to reflect the angle of the roof. With this done, glue and screw the sides onto the framework using 1½in (38mm) zinc-plated screws, inserted through pre-drilled holes.

Fig 3 Framework in position

To prepare the roof frames (which include the overhang) cut four lengths of batten, each about 16in (400mm) long. Cut 35° through the narrow section of one end of each piece (these pieces should lie 'flat'). Glue and screw together to form roof frames, using two further pieces of batten to brace the ridge (Fig 3). Glue and screw these frames to the sides with 1½in (38mm) zinc-plated screws inserted into side frames. When fixing these roof frames ensure that the sides are held at 90° to the base.

Fig 4 Securing tongue and groove cladding

Prepare cladding pieces for the back of the box and install these up to the roof line. For the front of the box, firstly prepare and join together three lengths of cladding; held firm away from the box, use a jig-saw, fret-saw or router to cut out an entrance hole 6–7in (150–175mm) wide by 9–10in (225–250mm) high (Fig 4). An entrance of this size will mean cutting through the complete width of one section of cladding; this will require some reinforcement on final assembly, by lining the inside of the hole with batten. Shape and join together the remaining two pieces of cladding, and secure the front cladding up to the roof line.

Prepare eight pieces of shiplap 39in (1m) long to clad the roof. Start with the *top* pieces and prepare a neat joint along the ridge by planing each edge to the appropriate angle (35°, 55°). To create a satisfactory join install a piece of batten along the inside of the ridge to accept screws. Plane this batten to the appropriate angle inside the roof.

Fig 5 Detail showing roof construction and 'fascia' trimming

Fig 6 Detail showing decorative ventilation holes and opaque white finish

Glue and screw roof cladding, using zinc-plated screws inserted into pre-drilled holes. Be sure to butt cladding accurately and evenly together. Trim the bottom pieces to provide the required overlap and thoroughly sand down all edges.

Prepare and secure a length of hardwood moulding to act as 'flashing' along the ridge, covering the joint of the two pieces of shiplap. Install a fascia board of ½×1½in (12×38mm) batten to the face of the roof (Fig 5) and drill decorative ventilation holes in the front and rear faces of the box (Fig 6). (This same 'facia' batten can also be used to conceal the ends of the side cladding.)

Thoroughly paint the whole structure with Sadolin Superdec or similar opaque white wood treatment. Be sure to treat the inside thoroughly too, either with Superdec or another coloured preservative stain.

Post/ramp Using tanalised timber build a slatted ramp of a length to suit your particular purpose. The ramp should extend into the water by at least 3in (75mm) at low water, and lie at a maximum angle of 35° to the water. This allows fowl to swim over the ramp before putting their feet down.

Fig 7 Post brackets and ramp assembly

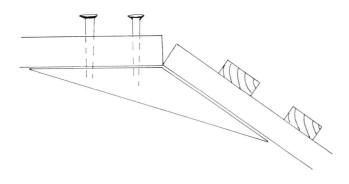

Fig 8 Ramp construction

The finished ramp should be secured to the underside of the nesting box with zinc-plated screws inserted through the base of the nest box down into the timbers supporting the ramp (see Figs 7 and 8).

Prepare four 45° brackets (Fig 7) for securing nesting box to post, using lengths of 2×2in (50×50mm) tanalised (sawn) timber. Two of the brackets should measure 12in (300mm) overall (for fixing across the *width* of the nesting box). Two of the brackets should measure 16in (400mm) overall (for fixing along the *length* of the nesting box). Pre-drill the ends of each bracket to accept 2½in (63mm) no 10/12 zinc-plated screws driven into both post and nesting-box base.

Prepare the supporting post and shape one end to a point to ease insertion. Re-treat this surface with Ensele, Protim or similar preservative suitable for ground-contact conditions.

Installation

The particular method of installation will depend on particular circumstances but the following procedure would normally be appropriate.

Insert post in required position, driving at least 39in (1m) into firm ground. If using a hammer protect the end-grain of the post with a block of heavy timber. Make sure that the post is vertical. With post almost in position remove any surplus damaged timber (and cut the post to its correct level) using a cross-cut saw. Pre-drill (with a hand-drill) through the top of the post to accept 2×2½in (50×63mm) no 10 zinc-plated screws, driven up into the base of the nest box. On NO ACCOUNT BRING POWER TOOLS ANYWHERE NEAR THE WATER.

Place box on post in 'balanced' position, with the post positioned slightly towards the rear of the base. Drive screws up through the post and into the base (if the screws protrude into the floor space turn small sections of waste batten onto them to conceal any sharp points).

Position and fix brackets (ensuring that the nesting box is level in all planes).

5 Oak bench

The traditional oak bench is commercially a thing of the past. The raw material is expensive and quality is difficult to control, at least in large-scale manufacture. The major garden furniture-makers use teak from plantations that they own, or control, in the Far East. This timber is of consistent quality and size and may be machined easily. The furniture is usually of high quality and often very attractive, but does not compare with an oak bench made from locally grown wood selected for its fine graining and colour. Such a bench will always be something special.

The back rail of the bench illustrated on p.105 is a fine example of the singular quality of oak. Cut on the 'quarter' the rail displays a phenomenon called the medulla – where the sheets of conducting tissues running radially through the vascular tissues of the tree are seen on the surface of the wood as silvery marks. Combined with the changes in colour of the rail this effect ensures that this piece of timber will be forever unique, and will always give a great deal of pleasure.

Oak is exceptionally durable, and provided that it is properly dried, will not warp or crack. As the years go by it just gets harder and harder. It is also a pleasure to work with. Unlike softwoods, if you chisel oak you actually get hard, straight edges *where you want them.*

The experience of making a piece of oak furniture is to be highly recommended. Even the novice woodworker will find the work straightforward and the wood forgiving.

BUYING OAK

This is the most important stage in making oak furniture and you should take your time looking at local suppliers, and asking local opinion, before deciding on a source of supply. You need to find a supplier who will select timber, and cut it, to suit your particular requirement. If you are lucky you will find one of those rare obsessionists who will insist on giving you a guided tour of all the interesting pieces of timber in his yard before settling on a piece that he considers right for your job.

Beware of going to large saw-mills as you may just be offered a 'slab' of oak, and it will be left to you to saw this to size.

Oak is sold by the cubic foot. The bench illustrated uses 3.2ft^3 (say 3.5ft^3) including waste. Be sure to ask potential suppliers what their price per cubic foot will be.

Manufacture

The cutting list in this project provides the opportunity for some flexibility in critical areas of design; before starting you should decide how high, wide and deep you wish your bench to be. The bench illustrated has a seat height of 17in (432mm), a seat depth of 19½in (495mm) and is 74in (1.88m) wide overall, but you may wish to change these dimensions to suit your own requirements.

Before starting construction, all the timber from the cutting list should be planed and sanded to remove saw marks and reveal the particular character of each piece. The 'look' of some of the capital pieces will decide their position in the bench as to whether they face forwards or backwards.

Plane with an electric plane on a low setting, .3 or .4mm. Be very careful not to gouge the large sections of timber along the edge of the plane's path. Always plane

along the grain and use long strokes, being sure to keep the plane moving all the time.

If you are uncertain about planing what can be very hard wood, you may consider it worthwhile to pay the extra and have your supplier plane the majority of pieces on the cutting list – it can be very hard work! Personally I find the planing operation very satisfying and, providing you are not too hasty, you should soon get the hang of it. It may be an idea to leave the really important planing work (that will show) until last.

MATERIALS

Oak bench with 6ft (1.8m) seat width
Back rail: 6×1½in (150×38mm), one 72in (1.8m) length
Seat rails: 4×1½in (100×38mm), two 72in (1.8m) lengths
Back slats: 1½×1in (38×25mm), twenty-one 15in (0.37m) lengths
Seat slats: 1½×1in (25×38mm), nine 72in (1.8m) lengths
Seat supports: 4×1½in (100×38mm), three 24in (0.60m) lengths
Rear legs: 3×6in (75×150mm), two 38in (0.95m) lengths
Front legs: 3×3in (75×75mm), two 28in (0.70m) lengths
Arms: 4×2in (100×50mm), two 24in (0.60m) lengths
Dowel: ½in (12.5mm), one length of 96in (2.4m)
Fixings: Tin of Cascamite resin glue (powder)
    Tube of plastic wood
    Raw linseed oil (not boiled)
    Forty-eight 2in (50mm) no 10 solid brass, countersunk screws
    Four 3in (75mm) no 12 solid brass screws

SPECIAL TOOLS

Circular saw
Electric plane
½in (13mm) and 1in (25mm) flat wood drill bits
Two large clamps 36in (915mm)
Two G clamps 6in (15cm)
Jig saw
Chisels, drill, bradawl, combination square, oil-stone etc

The Back

Take the 6×1½in (150×38mm) back rail and one of the 4×1½in (100×38mm) seat rails. Decide which face of each piece will face forwards and which therefore will be the *bottom* edge of the top rail and the *top* edge of the bottom rail – it is these edges that will receive mortice joints for the back slats. Establish the exact positions for twenty-one mortice joints (Fig 1) along each length of timber; also establish the extent of tenon joints at the end of each length.

Identify, and mark firmly with a bradawl or nail, the drill sites for producing mortice joints 1in (25mm) long by ½in (12.5mm) wide. Once these positions have been established, and you have checked for accuracy, begin drilling out the joints to a depth of 1½in (38mm) with a ½in (12.5mm) flat wood bit. See Figs 1 and 2. It is useful to wind a piece of coloured tape on the shank of the drill bit

Fig 1 Drilling out mortice joints having established positions

Fig 2 Finishing mortice joints with a chisel

to indicate the correct depth. Complete each mortice using a sharp chisel but leave the ends rounded – do *not* 'square' the joint. When all mortices are complete, plane the surfaces to remove pencil marks and blemishes.

Slats

Plane and prepare twenty-one 15in (375mm) pieces of 1× 1½in (25×38mm) oak – these will become back slats with a distance between shoulders (wood showing) of 12in (300mm). Mark and prepare two *tenon* joints on *one* piece (see Fig 3). The joints should measure ½in (12.5mm) wide × 1in (25mm) across × 1¼in (31mm) deep. With a sharp chisel and saw, 'round' the corners of the joint to reflect the rounded ends of the mortices already prepared. Test each joint in a mortice and, if satisfactory, use it as a pattern for the remaining twenty slats. It is critical that the shoulder length of each slat is identical. The shoulders of each tenon should close firmly on the morticed timber, and it is to ensure this that the tenons are ¼in (6mm) less deep than the mortices.

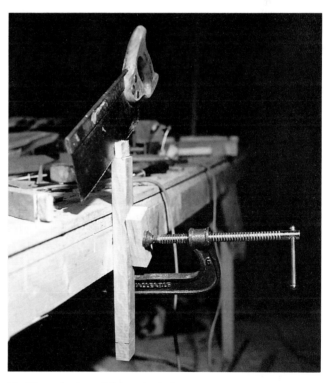

Fig 3 Preparing tenon joints on back slats

Tenons in Back Rails

It would be normal to prepare tenon joints on the ends of the back rails prior to assembly of the back, and if you are entirely confident of the spacing of slats etc, then this should now be done. Otherwise it may be left until the

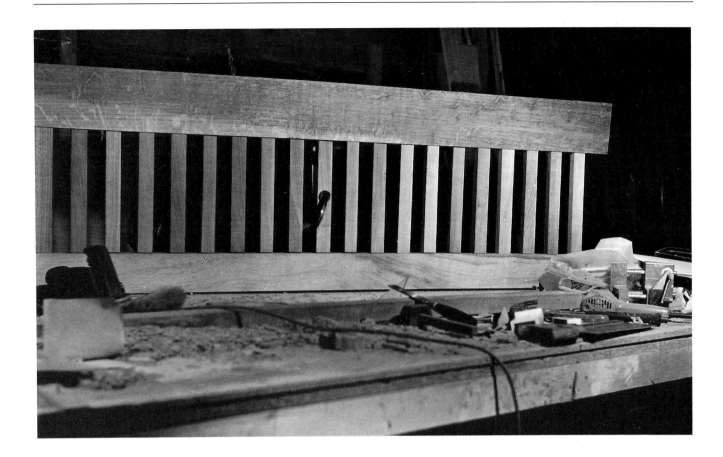

back assembly is complete (as in Fig 4). Tenons should be 1in (25mm) wide and 1½in (38mm) deep, with ½in (12.5mm) shoulders.

When all the slat joints are finished and each has been tested with its partner mortice, mix a quantity of Cascamite (following manufacturer's instructions) and use this on each tenon for final assembly. Fit the slats into one rail first, and then introduce to the second. Once all joints are located, clamp the completed assembly together (using blocks of wood between work and clamps) and leave for at least twelve hours. Remove surplus glue while still wet. Fig 4 shows the completed structure.

Legs, Armrest and Seat Support

Back legs. Figs 5 and 6 show the relationship of the back legs to the slatted back just completed. The large section of the timber (6×3in (150×75mm)) allows the back rest to be jointed in at an angle, for comfort, and it also provides strength and stability.

To create the reclining angle cut a wedge 2½×19in (63×475mm) from the two back legs (as in Fig 6). This may be done using a circular saw running along timber clamped to the workpiece. If the circular saw has not a deep enough cut the job should be finished with a cross-cut saw. Plane and finish the sawn edge.

Fig 4 Completed back assembly

Fig 5 Back assembly and seat support being jointed into leg

Fig 6 Armrest and seat assembly

Lay the two legs on a bench or level floor and marry the back assembly to them (Fig 5), using blocks of wood for support. Mark the positions for mortice joints to receive the tenons already made on the back rails. These should be parallel to the sloping front edge (Fig 5) and 2in (50mm) back from the front edge (to avoid interference with joint for seat rails). The mortices should be 1in (25mm) wide × 1¾in (44mm) deep and 5in (125mm) long for the top rail, and 1×1¾×3in (25×44×75mm) for the bottom rail. This will allow a ½in (12.5mm) shoulder at each end. Check and re-check that these joints are in the correct position before drilling; Fig 5 gives a good idea of position and angle.

When joints are complete, assemble the back and legs. Do not glue or secure in any way.

Seat Supports (Outside)

Take two of the 24in (600mm) lengths of 4×1½in (100× 38mm) timber. Assess the depth of seat required, and what the span between front and back legs needs to be to achieve this. Allow for two 1½in (38mm) tenons and trim any surplus from each length. Mark and cut tenons in the ends of each support 3in (75mm) long × 1in (25mm) wide × 1½in (38mm) deep. Use a jig-saw to create a slight curve in the upper surface of the seat supports (Fig 6 shows this clearly). A spokeshave may be used to good effect to clean up this concave surface. The curve will greatly improve comfort.

Drill and chisel a mortice in each back leg to receive the seat support timber (see Fig 5). Now remove the back assembly from the back legs, and measure and joint the remaining timbers – see Fig 6. Be very careful to assess the height of the armrests for your own comfort, and be particularly accurate in forming the joints from armrests to back legs.

Dowelling

When the arm/leg assemblies are complete to your satisfaction, glue and dowel each joint as shown in Fig 7. To dowel successfully follow this procedure:

1 Clamp joints tightly wherever possible.
2 Ensure a 90° angle (if appropriate) between components.
3 Drill through the mortice and tenon. If using a flat wood bit, remember that the leading point of the bit drives in some way ahead of the intended measurement. This may mean that the bit will break surface on the 'wrong' side of the work. If this happens withdraw the bit, and drill in from the 'wrong' side to complete the hole. If you push a flat wood bit through a piece of timber it will cause a lot of damage on 'exit'. If unsure of this point test drill through some scrap timber. You will soon see what I mean.

Ideally the dowel should cross from one side of the mortice into the other, passing completely through the tenon.
4 Cut a piece of dowel at least ½in (12.5mm) longer than required and smooth and round one end. This will assist in starting the dowel into the object hole and will also prevent tearing of the wood on exit (if required to exit).

Fig 7 Jointing and dowelling front legs

5 Firmly drive the dowel home, having first assessed how far it needs to go.

6 Saw or chisel away the waste end and smooth with plane or sandpaper.

After dowelling the arm/leg assemblies, test them for accuracy and stability by fitting to the back. The inside of each front leg should then be morticed to accept the front seat support (Fig 7), which also requires preparation. This component should be identical to the bottom rail of the back assembly.

Central Seat Support

Assemble the completed components of the bench but *do not* fix. *Assess* and mark the positions for mortices to hold the central seat support (shown in Fig 8). With the greatest care measure the span required for the support, and be particularly careful in taking into account the reclining

Fig 8 Showing central seat support in position

angle of the back. The mortice and tenon joints should be quite shallow, say ½in (12.5mm), and should be reinforced on final assembly with 3in (75mm) countersunk brass screws (no 12) driven through front and back rails.

Final Assembly

When you are happy that all joints are correct and flush, glue and dowel the completed bench components. Dowels securing the back top rail to legs should be driven from the rear, so that they do not show on the 'good' side of the back legs.

Seat Slats

Plane and prepare eight or nine seat slats to span the three seat supports. Lay the timber across the supports to assess position and use a convenient block of wood as a spacer during fixing. One slat should be secured directly over the front seat rail (see Fig 9) and another should be secured as

Fig 9 Positioning and securing seat slats on completed structure

far back as possible. Secure each slat with six countersunk 2in (50mm) no 10 brass screws driven into pre-drilled and countersunk holes. Fill each screw site with plastic wood, or, for neatness and finish, a wooden plug.

Treatment

Thoroughly clean the whole finished bench with a cloth impregnated with white spirit to remove pencil marks and dust. Paint all timber with raw linseed oil, and leave to stand out of the sunlight for at least one week before moving to its site. Further applications of raw linseed oil should be made over the course of the next few weeks.

A NOTE ABOUT THE CARVING

As you will have observed, this particular bench was made to commemorate the life and death of Jack and Betty Richardson. The client for whom this was made initially requested a brass plate, but I felt that a carved inscription would be far nicer, particularly in combination with the highly unusual back rail.

The beautifully balanced, sharp lettering was carved by a friend, Peter Williams, who lives just across the meadow from me in Bungay, Suffolk. He is an artist and stone mason, but was very pleased to have the opportunity to get his eye in with some lettering on oak.

The carving process is very exacting, requiring a great deal of preparation work leading up to the transfer of a pencil tracing directly onto the wood, before carving can even start. Great care has to be taken in the carving, since the slightest slip of the chisel could be disastrous. It is certainly not something to be recommended for the amateur.

6 Picnic table

One picnic table of this type could be said to be very much like another. They all share the same design features and function and are certainly among the more utilitarian pieces of garden furniture that you are likely to find. With the table illustrated below I have tried to soften its somewhat harsh impression by producing an interesting slatted surface and with the sympathetic use of colour. Before you rush out to buy a vibrant redwood stain to splash onto a piece of furniture it is worth considering the impact of this colour on your garden – you may find that there is nothing else at all with which it is remotely in sympathy. A shade such as the 'walnut' used in the illustration will be reflected in the colours of tree bark, rose-woods etc, and will help the table to 'withdraw', in a design sense, into the overall garden landscape.

MATERIALS

4×2in (100×50mm) tanalised sawn softwood,
   four 6ft (1.8m) lengths (legs)
2×2in (50×50mm) tanalised sawn softwood,
   three 4ft (1.22m) lengths (top and seat bearers)
   one 7ft (2.14m) length (bracing spar)
1½×1½in (38×38mm) PSE (planed square edge),
   twelve 51in (1.3m) length (slats)
   one 24in (600mm) length (central top support)
7×1½in (175×38mm) tanalised PSE,
   two 54in (1.37m) length (seats)
Fixings: Twenty 2in (50mm) no 8 zinc-plated screws (cross-head)
Sixteen 2½in (63mm) no 10 zinc-plated screws (cross-head)
Four 3in (75mm) no 10/12 zinc-plated screws
Twenty-four 3in (75mm) galvanised nails
Preservative wood treatment/stain (Sadolin, Cuprinol etc)

SPECIAL TOOLS

360° Protractor

Construction

The Legs Take a 6ft (1.8m) length of 4×2 (100×50mm) tanalised timber and remove a 35° wedge from one end (each leg will make an angle of 55° to the ground – see Fig 1a). Measure 34in (864mm) from the new corner and replicate the first cut in the same plane. You should now have a leg, which, when placed on the ground as in final installation, presents a top surface parallel to the ground. Use this finished leg as a template for the production of three more.

Prepare two 24in (600mm) lengths of 2×2in (50×50mm) tanalised sawn timber and establish the centre point of each (12in, 300mm). Lay two legs on the bench and abut them to the centre point of one of these timbers, as they would seat in the completed article (Figs 2 and 3).

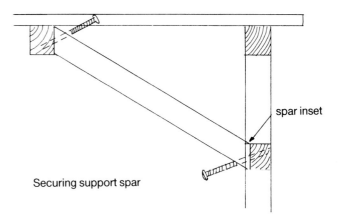

Fig 1b Support construction

Prepare a 48in (1.22m) length of 2×2in (50×50mm) tanalised timber and lay this onto the legs to describe a seat bearer with its top surface 17in (432mm) from the ground. Mark the positions clearly and create a 1in (25mm) angled half-lap joint in each leg to accept the seat bearer (see Fig 3). Use a tenon saw and chisel to prepare the joints.

When complete, reassemble the A-frame and secure through the top bearer, down into the legs, with two 3in (75mm) zinc screws. Secure the seat bearer with two 2½in (63mm) zinc screws per joint. Pre-drill all screws holes. Repeat operation for second A-frame.

Be sure to treat all concealed surfaces (where joints have been made in tanalised timber) with a fresh application of preservative before securing joint.

Table-top Lay twelve 51in (1.3m) lengths of 1½×1½in (38×38mm) PSE onto a level surface so that the ends are precisely level with each other. Establish the centre point of the two outside slats and draw a line between these across all the slats to define the position for the central

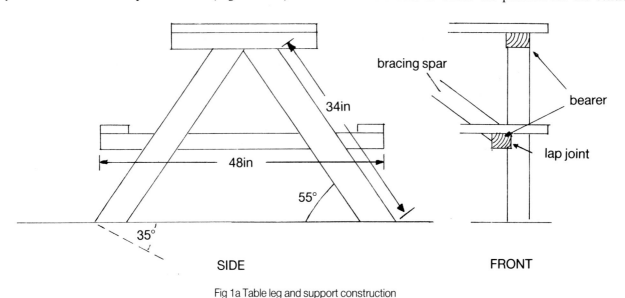

Fig 1a Table leg and support construction

Fig 1 Construction of table top, showing position of central support

Fig 3 Assembly at the site

Fig 2 Trial assembly of table top and legs

table-top support (Fig 1) made from one length (24in, 600mm) of 1½×1½in (38×38mm) PSE.

Secure the two outside table slats to abut each end of this central support, using 2in (50mm) zinc screws through pre-drilled holes. Secure remaining slats between them after first establishing an even spacing. Be sure that the ends of the slats lie absolutely level, so as to accept a trimming piece of 1½×1½in (38×38mm) laid against them (Fig 1) – it may help to secure the trimming pieces to the ends of the outside slats before in-filling with remaining slats. Secure slats to trimming pieces with 3in (75mm) galvanised nails, driven through pre-drilled holes. (Remember, nailing into the end grain may split the wood, so go carefully!) Nail-holes may be countersunk and filled with waterproof wood filler if required.

Sand any rough edges thoroughly and slightly chamfer the edges of the trimming pieces with a plane, if you are able. Be careful to remove any remaining sharp corners, which could be dangerous for children.

Assembly With table-top and A-frames complete, you now need to assess the position for two bracing spars to span from the centre of the seat bearers to the centre of the central table-top bearer. The positioning of one of these spars may be seen in Figs 2 and 3.

Lay the completed table-top face down on the bench and position an A-frame on it, about 3–4in (75–100mm) from the edge (Fig 2, and 3). The seat bearer should be on the 'inside' of the A-frame. Assess the dimensions and angles required for a bracing spar of 2×2in (50×50mm) tanalised timber, which should be cut into the seat bearer with a shallow ½in (12mm) joint (see Figs 1a and 1b). Be sure that the A-frame is held at precisely 90° to the table-top during this procedure.

Produce two bracing spars and check that all the components of the table will fit together, once at the site.

Lastly, prepare two 54in (1.37m) lengths of 7×1½in (175×38mm) timber for the seats. These should be thoroughly sanded and pre-drilled to accept no 10 zinc-plated screws as shown in Fig 4.

Apply a wood stain/treatment to the components either now, or after assembly, and remember particularly to treat any concealed surfaces prior to assembly. Refer to the

Fig 4 Securing plank seats

manufacturers' instructions when painting untreated wood. Tanalised timbers may be coloured with just one coat.

Remove components to the site and secure the A-frames and bracing spars to the table-top with 2½in (63mm) zinc-plated screws driven through pre-drilled holes into the underside of the table-top and central support. Use four screws in table-top and two in central support.

Finally secure each seat with two 2in (50mm) screws at each end (Fig 4), deeply countersunk and driven through pre-drilled holes into seat bearers.

7 Tree house/play centre

When my first child was old enough to start using swings and slides we started to look at the range and price of garden activity centres. They were mainly 'climbing frame' structures with ladders, steps and slides attached, and were very expensive – I refused to give any of them garden room on the grounds of expense, safety and design. Instead I built our own small activity centre, incorporating a second-hand slide, around an old apple tree. This gave immense enjoyment to my daughters and their friends, whilst I was more satisfied with its safety and design.

Tree house nearing completion

The play centre illustrated is a more finished version of the original structure; its semi-enclosed design provides the opportunity for many uses, one being a club house in which the children can have their picnic teas and hold their secret meetings.

Not everyone is lucky enough to have an old twisted tree with lots of low boughs around which a play centre may be built – a free-standing structure, perhaps with young trees or shrubs planted around it, will serve the children just as well.

In the design I felt it important to ensure that any child who fell could only fall onto grass and not, as could happen with some climbing frames, risk injury on steel tubes on the way down. I also wanted to avoid the 'bottleneck' which steep steps on a garden slide can cause when one of the children in a group is slow to get up the ladder. I have therefore not used a slide ladder, but installed a long, gently sloping ramp up into the tree house, and an easy step up to the slide from there.

The tree house is so much part of the tree that it does not intrude into the overall garden plan in the way that a free-standing climbing frame could do. Using wood allows the application of wood treatments and stains in colours sympathetic to the garden environment – the only thing you may have little control over is the colour of the slide.

As the children get older I intend to attach rather more adventurous activities to the basic structure, such as rope-walks or a 'Zip' wire to the ground in place of the slide. In this way the structure will probably have a useful life of nine or ten years; if I had bought a standard climbing frame, it may well have been mothballed after just a year or two, as the children outgrew it.

MATERIALS

The quantity of materials needed will obviously depend on the particular size and design of your play centre. In general I would recommend the use of the following types of material for the specific applications shown.

Base frames/posts: 3×3in (75×75mm), or 2×2in (50×50mm) tanalised sawn timber (see text p.55)
Floors: ¾×5in (19×125mm) tongue and groove
Cladding (side): ¾×5in (19×125mm) shiplap; or tongue and groove, V or matching
Cladding (roof): ¾×5in (19×125mm) shiplap
Ramp: Two 6×1½in (150×38mm) tanalised sawn plank
Corner braces: 1½×1½in (38×38mm) PSE batten
Roof frames: 1×1½in (25×38mm) PSE batten
Galvanised nails and zinc-plated screws
No special tools are required, although the use of an electric jig-saw will certainly speed things up.

The construction of this item is dealt with in quite general terms, as it is anticipated that you will wish to build a structure to fit round a particular tree, or conform to a particular site in some way. Your particular design will be motivated by the age of children and the type of activities you wish to offer. For example, incorporating a slide will dictate the necessary height of the raised floor.

You may also like to consider a moveable structure, which can be moved round the garden as the grass below it and round about gets worn and/or discoloured.

Fig 1 Tree house floor

The Raised Floor

The raised floor of the tree house (Fig 1) is a simple framework of 2×2in (50×50mm) tanalised timber, clad with ¾×5in (19×125mm) tongue and groove boards and supported by the tree trunk or boughs, or, where this support is not available, by posts of 2×2in (50×50mm) (or larger) timber. The tree house illustrated derives most of its support and rigidity from the tree itself, so I could use relatively slender 2×2in (50×50mm) supporting posts, set into the ground, for minor additional support. In circumstances where rather less support is available from the tree it would be wise to use 3×3in (75×75mm) tanalised posts, and these should be set into some form of concrete foundation if there is any likelihood of the structure being subject to sideways movement.

Where posts are required they should continue upwards to provide a framework for the wall cladding (Fig 2). This

Fig 2 Constructing a timber framework for the wall cladding

work is best done at the site unless you can be sure of the eventual dimensions.

First make the outer framework with simple nailed joints and use long galvanised nails to secure into tree wood where necessary (these nails will not hurt the tree if used in moderation). Corners supported by posts should be jointed into these posts to provide a firm, cohesive structure, and secured with zinc-plated screws inserted through pre-drilled holes. Before jointing ensure that the posts are driven firmly into the ground. In particularly soft ground, it may be advisable to provide some form of foundation.

It is useful to bear in mind that the growth of the tree may distort the structure in future years. With this in mind try to anticipate changes that may be required and, for example, avoid securing into wood that is obviously still developing at a measurable rate. You will also be wise (unlike me!) to ensure that the floor is square or rectangular – this will facilitate the installation of roof cladding and give a neat finish to wall cladding at the corners.

Once the outer framework is established and secured into position fit in additional supports to ensure that there will be no unsupported span of floor-board longer than 3ft (1m), and begin laying floorboards from one corner or edge to the other, at 90° to any underfloor supports. Be sure to lay all the boards the same way up. Some types of tongue and groove are not quite central in the section of timber and you may not notice that one board is slightly

raised until it is too late. Trim each board as you go along with a jig-saw or cross-cut saw.

If the boards are untreated at this stage, you should apply a wood treatment to any areas that will be hidden from the brush after assembly (ie overlaps onto frames).

When complete, test the floor yourself to ensure that it is strong and stable enough for your children. You should be able to jump up and down on it with impunity.

Side Frames

As in Fig 2 decide on the wall height and configuration and build a framework of timber to accept cladding. Buttress these frames with short lengths of $1\frac{1}{2}\times1\frac{1}{2}$in (38×38mm) batten (or similar), with each end cut at 45° to sit flush against floor and frame. Secure these buttresses with long galvanised nails or zinc-plated screws driven through pre-drilled holes. Fit roof plates across two sides with their upper surfaces either planed or in some way jointed to the corner posts, to present a flush surface to the roof at its intended pitch (say 45°) – Figs 2 and 3. Ensure that the distances between corner posts is the same top and bottom.

The Roof

With the side frames finished you should now be able to measure up for the roof (and build this in your workshop for fitting complete) – see Fig 3. Aim for a steep roof pitch (say 45°) to provide plenty of internal headroom, and make

Fig 3 Roof assembly

two simple frames from lengths of 1×1½in (25×38mm) batten, or similar. Secure these frames with a simple cross-piece near the apex and a glued and screwed joint *at* the apex. Test the frames in position to ensure fitting, and be sure to provide a small overlap (say 4in (100mm)) to carry rainwater well away from the walls. Decide how you will fix these frames to the corner posts (zinc screws through sides of frames into posts?), and measure the required span of roof cladding.

Measure and cut lengths of cladding (shiplap) and secure, starting from the bottom of the roof, with wood glue and galvanised nails (1¼in, 31mm) – pre-drill

Fig 4 Fitting cladding

through cladding for nails. At the ridge cut cladding along its length to fit as closely as possible and flash with a piece of hardwood moulding or similar. You may consider positioning an additional frame along the inside of the ridge, to which the last pieces of cladding and the flashing may be secured.

Place the roof in position and secure to corner posts, and the angled roof plates you have already positioned, with zinc-plated screws, through pre-drilled holes.

Walls

Decide on the required configuration of walls and the position of slides, steps, or other entrances. If required build in additional frames eg 'doorway' for slide (Fig 4) around these points and begin applying cladding from the bottom, using galvanised nails into pre-drilled holes. Provide a flush joint at corner posts, with the cladding from one wall matching up to the cladding on the next (see illustration on p.97). You may wish to flash the corner joints with a piece of hardwood moulding. Reinforce any windows that you may install with a simple framework of batten, screwed to the cladding from the inside, and be sure to sand down any exposed surfaces thoroughly. Secure with zinc-plated screws any cladding that may be exposed to particular pressure, such as being leant on or relied on for support in some way.

Fig 5 The ramp

Ramp

Fig 5 shows the general construction of a long ramp, leading onto the raised floor. Ideally this should be of tanalised, sawn planks butted together to provide at least 12in (300mm) of walking width. The planks should be firmly nailed or screwed onto the floor frame, and embedded into the ground. If additional support is required this should be provided by lengths of 2×2in (50× 50mm) timber driven into the ground on either side of the ramp and connected with a spar of timber running laterally underneath the ramp. If you are in any doubt about the firmness of the handrail support posts, then for safety's sake it will be wise to concrete these in. Any timber protruding above the level of the ramp should be trimmed flush, so that it cannot be tripped over. Set a handrail at a convenient height (say 24in (600mm)) and a few inches to one side of the ramp in a position that will allow children to walk up the centre of the planks while

holding the rail (if you secure a handrail flush with the side of the ramp children will be forced to walk on the edge of the ramp). Be sure that the handrail (2×2in (50×50mm)) is planed and sanded smooth before use. Your local timber merchant will probably have some moulded handrail in stock if you are feeling rich.

Give the ramp a gradient of about 1 in 3 (30°), and you may consider securing some heavy-duty wire mesh (galvanised) to the surface to prevent slipping in wet or icy weather. If you do this make sure that you are not replacing one hazard with another by leaving raised wires on the ramp – on balance I feel it may be better for children to fall on their bottoms on a slippery surface than on their teeth after falling over wire.

Ladder

A simple ladder may be made (see Fig 6) using two lengths of 2×2in (50×50mm) tanalised timber with rungs of 1in (25mm) hardwood dowel inserted into pre-drilled holes.

Wood Treatment/Stain

Use a product such as Sadolin or Cuprinol to thoroughly treat and stain all timber. Use a darker shade for roof than for walls to give a more house-like appearance.

Fig 6 The ladder

8 Cottage dovecote

The dovecote illustrated in this chapter is a model which I have been making commercially for some years. The prototype was made for my mother-in-law, whose rather plain dove 'box' had started to disintegrate. She was unable to find an attractive replacement and I offered to design one for her. In researching for design ideas I looked at a variety of other dovecotes which revealed that the quality of design for aesthetic purposes was very poor. The range went from very pretty but tiny dovecotes on enormous pillars, to uninspiring rustic examples tacked onto trees. In no case did I see a dovecote which looked as though it had been designed to feature in the overall garden plan.

The Cottage dovecote is of complex design and each stage of its manufacture requres careful consideration. This complexity is one of the prices to be paid for the aesthetic quality of the design, and I make no apologies for it.

The principle of manufacture in this project is the production of wall and roof sections of identical size, which will fit precisely together in final assembly. The specific dimensions are relatively unimportant, and may be changed to suit a particular requirement. The effect of changes on the overall balance and design of the structure should, however, be very carefully considered.

This project deals with the production of a free-standing dovecote; the next (p.117) discusses the adaptation of this design for wall mounting, following the same principles of manufacture but varying the number of sides and applications. Materials used in this project should be of good quality, planed to a fine finish. Any attempt to use substandard material, such as larch-lap, is bound to result in a disappointing product.

MATERIALS

Eight compartment, free-standing octagonal dovecote

¾×5in (19×125mm) tongue and groove 'V' or 'matching' softwood
    49ft (15m) in six 8ft 4in (2.5m) lengths (side cladding)
¾×5in (19×125mm) shiplap softwood
    36ft (11m) in various lengths (roof cladding, landing stages)
1×1½in (25×38mm) planed square edge softwood
    80ft (24m) (batten: frames, etc)
1×5in (25×125mm) tongue and groove softwood
    27ft (8m) in long lengths (base)
    16ft (4.8m) birdsmouth (or similar) hardwood moulding
2×2in (50×50mm) tanalised (sawn) timber
    7ft 4in (2.2m) (post brackets)
4×4in (100×100mm) tanalised (sawn) timber
    12ft (3.6m) in one length (post)
One sheet ¼in (6mm) exterior ply (compartment 'walls')

Fixings: 72 × no 8 1½in (38mm) zinc plated screws (cross head)
1lb (½ kilo) × 1¼in (31mm) narrow (small head) galvanised nails
Six 3in (75mm) no 10/12 zinc-plated screws
Waterproof resin wood glue
Colour/Treatment: Clear preservative
Opaque white wood treatment or microporous paint system
Scrap timber for jigs and templates

SPECIAL TOOLS

Circular saw with angle attachment (to 45°)
Jig-saw
Router or fret-saw
Clamp
360° protractor

Manufacture

The base: The dovecote base is an arrangement of 1×5in (25×125mm) tongue and groove timber, cut into an octagonal shape, with the longest dimension being 39in (1m). With reference to Fig 1 place lengths of tongue and groove together in such a way that you can mark out a circle of 39in (1m) diameter – you will need to use nine widths of timber to do this properly. *Do not* be tempted to reduce the diameter slightly so as to use only eight widths. When satisfied that you can draw the circle, establish the centre point (on the fifth board) and make a mark 7¾in (194mm) either side of this point *along* the length of the board. Lay two 41in (1025mm) lengths of 1×1½in (25×38mm) batten at 90° to the run of timber so that the two marks just made define the *internal* distance between these battens. Lay them with their narrow (1in (25mm)) dimension against the base boards. The role of these battens is to tie in and strengthen the base timber.

Fig 1 Preparation of dovecote base

When you have checked that the battens are equidistant apart along their length, and at exactly 90° to the run of boards, mark their positions with a pencil line. Make a further mark at the end of each at the point where they span the 'outside' boards. Pre-drill through these marks for four no 8 screws (1½in (38mm)). These screws will serve to hold the boards together during nailing. Glue along the length of each batten and re-site along pencil lines. Screw down one end of each and firmly draw boards together before securing other ends.

Turn the assembly over and draw a line along the path of each batten to enable accurate nailing. Drive 1¼in (31mm) galvanised nails through pre-drilled holes through the boards into the batten (two nails per board into each batten).

At all times during this project ensure that cladding or other softwood timber is pre-drilled to accept nails; this will avoid the wood splitting, particularly near the end grain.

Fig 2 Using jig saw to cut out base

Fig 3 Using a template to prepare side frame timbers

When the assembly is securely nailed re-establish the centre point on the new surface (perhaps by drilling through with a small bit) and then draw in the circle again (39in (1m) diameter). Fig 1 illustrates one way of doing this by nailing a slat of wood to the centre point and holding a pencil through a hole drilled at the correct radius.

Using a 360° protractor, draw lines across the circle to divide it into eight 45° segments. Make sure that four of the 'points' of the octagon lie directly above each end of the two base battens. This will ensure that the first and last sections of tongue and groove are completely supported (this can just be seen in Fig 2, and also in Fig 7).

Check that the measurement between the lines crossing the circle is consistent and then join these points to define an octagon.

With a jig-saw (preferably) cut round this shape (Fig 2) and thoroughly sand the edges.

The sides: Each of the eight sides is made from two pieces of 1×1½in (25×38mm) batten (frame) spanned by six pieces of tongue and groove (V or matching) board. The frames and board edges are angled at 22½° to fit their partners. Accuracy is essential for this system to work properly.

Preparing Frames

For cutting pieces of 1×1½in (25×38mm) batten along their length to the correct angle refer to Template 2 on p.50. In the first instance cut 35ft (10.5m) of timber to 22½° (you may need to prepare more, depending on waste).

With reference to Figs 3 and 3a prepare a simple jig to cut each side frame to an exact length, and to cut an angle in the top of each which will provide a seat for roof section frames (see Fig 3b). The correct angle is 35° (to the horizontal). Frames should be cut to a longest dimension of 24½in (612mm) (to tip of angled end).

Use the jig to prepare eight left-hand and eight right-hand frames. Details of how to differentiate between the two may be found in Figs 3a and 3b.

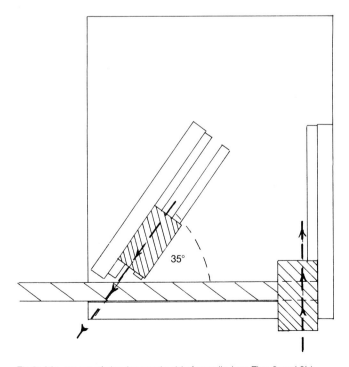

Fig 3a Movement of circular saw in side frame jig (see Figs 3 and 3b)

(*opposite*) Oak bench (Project 5)
(*overleaf on p.106*) Tree house/play centre (Project 6)

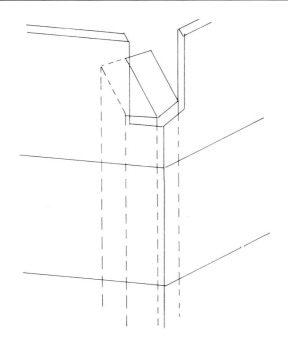

Fig 3b Section showing left and right-hand side frames joined, and piece of cladding removed, to create seat for roof frames

Cladding

Refer to Template 1 on p.48 (and see Fig 4); following the method described, you should be able to produce eight sides with edges angled at 22½° and measuring 11in (275mm) across externally. Each of the sides should be made with six lengths of ¾×5in (19×125mm) tongue and groove 'V' (matching) softwood. The bottom piece of each side should have its groove removed, using a circular saw or plane, to provide a flush seat to the dovecote base.

Fig 4 Using a template to prepare side frame cladding

Assembly of Frames and Cladding

Although not essential you will find it worthwhile to make a simple jig for assembly of side components. The use of this jig may be seen in Fig 5 and its production is explained in Jig 1 (p.50). Its role is to provide a secure and accurate seat for components during gluing and nailing.

Lay left- and right-hand frames in the jig so that the angled edges lie face up and ready to accept cladding pieces laid flush on them. Glue along each length and put the bottom piece of cladding (with groove removed) into the jig and pull down firmly against the base. Pre-drill, at each end of cladding pieces, for two 1¼in (31mm) galvanised nails, and insert nails being careful to follow the angle at which the frames lie in the jig. When the first piece is secure lay on, and pull down, the remaining pieces and secure in the same way. The last piece should be secured with a single nail placed in such a way that it will not interfere when the corner of each cladding piece is cut out to expose the angled roof frame seat (see Fig 3b).

When one side is complete check that its detail is accurate and, in particular, that the 35° roof seat angles are the right way round (check against Figs 3a and 3b). Make any necessary adjustments to the jig before completing the remaining sides.

Fig 5 A jig for assembly of side components for wall sections – see Jig 1 (p51) for details

Entrance Holes

You should now form entrance holes in each of the eight sides, four at low level and four more at high level (see Fig 7 and p.107). Each hole should measure 4in (100mm) across and 7in (175mm) high (max) and should be cut into the

Fig 6 Template for router

Landing Stages

Fig 6a shows the construction and installation of landing stages required for the four upper level entrances. Use 11in (275mm) lengths of shiplap, flat side up and with the 'lap' removed. Triangular supporting pieces should be cut from waste tongue and groove (from the base construction) so that the grain is running in the same direction as the hypotenuse ie at approximately 45° to the vertical side (see also p.107).

You should now have a completed base and eight sides, which will require trimming before roof installation. This is best done with the body of the dovecote complete.

Assembly of Dovecote Body

Cut eight pieces of 1×1½in (25×38mm) batten 8in (203mm) long and pre-drill holes for no 8 screws approximately 1in (25mm) from either end (through narrow section). These pieces will be screwed to the base and, in turn, receive the sides (Fig 7). With reference to the existing pencil marks on the base assess the correct position for the dovecote sides. Provided the lines are accurate these positions will be self-evident, but be sure that the sides are parallel with the edges of the base.

Mark the position of a side with a line drawn along its *inside* edge. This line will enable the correct positioning of a piece of batten, which should now be glued and screwed into position, centrally between segment lines. Pre-drill two screw holes at the bottom of the cladding (to secure side to batten) and two screw holes 4in (100mm) from the top and bottom of *one* side frame, at an angle that will allow secure fixing to the next frame *and* access for a screwdriver.

Glue the bottom edge of cladding as well as the inside edge where it will abut the secured batten, and then re-locate and secure the first side section. Repeat the process for each side, alternating the high and low entrances. Use a clamp to hold side pieces in the correct position while screwing together.

With the structure assembled use a tenon saw and broad chisel to remove a section of cladding over each corner, thus creating a seat for the roof frames. In final assembly the roof frames should abut the side frames neatly. Fig 3b shows the piece removed, and the seat in side frames which will receive roof frames.

Fill any imperfect joints with linseed oil putty and thoroughly sand down all edges.

first and second cladding pieces (lower level) and fourth and fifth cladding pieces (higher level) so that the hole is central to the cladding pieces and from side to side (Fig 7). It is very important that no cladding piece is cut through its entire width.

To form the holes either produce a template for a router (Fig 6), or cut the required shape in a piece of ply, draw round this shape on the object wood, and cut with a jig-saw or fret-saw. Sand down all sawn edges thoroughly.

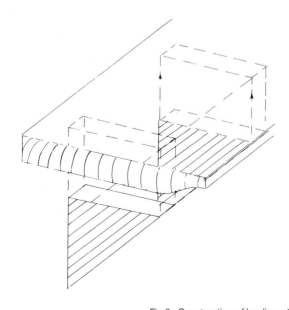

Fig 6a Construction of landing-stage

Roof Sections

The dovecote roof is made in the same way as wall sections, with cladding spanning two frame pieces. It is,

Fig 7 Assembly of sides of base

however, a far more awkward operation and you should be sure that you understand the relevant sections in Chapter 3, General Construction Principles before making a start.

Preparing Roof Frames

As with side frames you need to prepare lengths of 1× 1½in (25×38mm) batten, cut at an angle. For an octagonal roof pitched at 35° each frame needs to be angled at 13½° (as close as possible) along its length (see Multi-Facet Structures p.47 for the maths behind this statement). Refer to Template 2 (p.50) for guidance in preparing this timber. Prepare 35ft (10.5m) in the first instance, and cut into sixteen 24in (600mm) lengths. At a later stage these

pieces will need to be shaped to fit together at the apex of the roof. It is possible to produce a jig for this operation but so complicated as to be not worthwhile for production of a single model.

Roof Cladding

Each roof section is made from five pieces of ¾×5in (19× 125mm) shiplap. The lap helps to ensure removal of rainwater and, coupled with a suitably waterproof painting system, provides a sound, waterproof roof.

Using the same principle as with production of side

Fig 8 Template for production of roof cladding

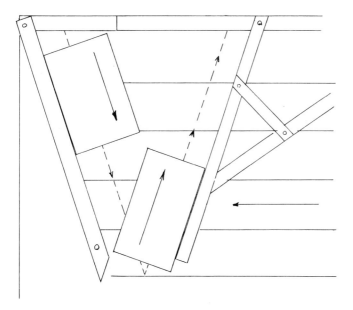

Fig 8a Plan of roof section template showing direction of travel for circular saw and style of construction

cladding prepare a template (Figs 8 and 8a) to produce eight sections of roof cladding. The template should control the passage of a circular saw, with cutting angle set at 13½°, in cutting a triangular section of cladding. The triangle should have an apex angle of 36.5° and base angles of 71.75° and span five pieces of shiplap.

You may choose to prepare these sections in some other way, such as by laying single pieces onto a jig, with side frames installed, and cutting each piece to fit in-situ. This may not be so accurate but it is perfectly acceptable and may be easier.

Assembly of Roof Frames and Cladding

As with side pieces you should now produce a jig in which to hold the roof frames and cladding secure during gluing and nailing. Reference to Jig 2 on p.52 will give you a guide for manufacture but the specifics of that section relate to cutting of cladding in-situ (for larger structures such as pergola and summerhouse). If you have used a template to produce triangular roof sections accurately, then your jig should be made as in Figs 5 and 9 *ie* to accept shaped pieces into a defined form. The jig should accurately reflect the shape of prepared pieces, with apex angle 36.5°.

When you have produed a satisfactory jig place a frame

Fig 9 Jig for assembly of roof components

Fig 10 Roof assembly

component into it and assess the angle at which it should be cut, so as to fit its partner at the apex. Repeat the procedure for the other sides and for the remaining frame sections.

Now lay frames into jig, glue along their lengths and apply cladding, starting from the apex and working down. Be sure to butt the shiplap tightly and consistently. Pre-drill cladding and secure as with side sections. Check accuracy on completion of first panel and adjust jig if required. Do not trim any timber from the bottom of complete sections until later.

Assembly of Completed Roof Sections

Lay two completed roof sections face down on the bench so that they are aligned at the apex. Pre-drill two screw holes through one frame approximately 4in (100mm) from either end and drive screws through to draw sections together. Fig 10 shows this clearly. Repeat until all eight sections come together to form the complete roof. A small clamp may be useful during this operation.

Turn roof right-way-up and fill any imperfect joints with linseed oil putty, after first sanding down rough edges. Using a circular saw or jig-saw trim round the edge of the roof (remove about 1½in (38mm)). Ideally the finished roof should measure 23in (575mm) from apex to edge, measured along the frame.

Each joint should now be covered with a piece of 'birdsmouth' or similar hardwood moulding glued and nailed (through pre-drilled holes) into the frames. The moulding should come to a point at the apex of the roof. If you find that you are left with a hole at the apex fill this with a well-worked mixture of sawdust and wood glue, rather than putty, as it may be required to accept a brass or wooden 'dolly', installed as a final embellishment.

Fitting Roof to Body

By positioning the completed roof over the body you will now be able to assess how much trimming of the side cladding is required. Saw through and chisel out cladding to open roof/side joints (see Fig 3b), and then trim surplus cladding until roof sits accurately all round. Remove roof

Fig 11a Construction and assembly of exterior ply compartment dividers

and sand down all rough edges, both on roof and body.

At a later stage you will need to screw the roof to the body. This is best done using four 1½in no 8 zinc screws inserted upwards from the inside of the dovecote through the side frames and into the roof frames. You will be able to put your arm through an upper entrance hole to drive an already positioned screw into position, if that screw is inserted *two* frames to the right (left-handed) or *two* frames to the left (right-handed). Do not do this until you have produced and installed the inserts defining compartment spaces.

Plywood Inserts

With reference to Fig 11a prepare plywood inserts dividing the lower and upper floors into four compartments separated by a floor. Fig 11 shows the completed inserts in position.

The 'walls' should span from the inside corner of one side frame to the opposing inside corner of the opposite frame, the two parts being slotted together to form a cross (see Fig 11a). Cut-in in this way they should require no further fixing. The floor should be cut to drop more or less precisely into the internal space and sit on the lower space

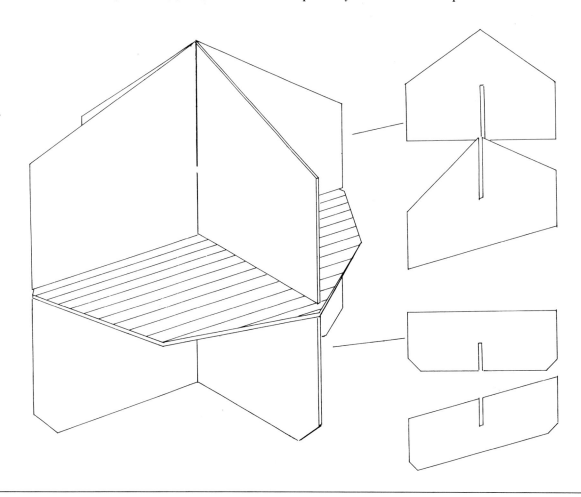

Fig 11 Plywood inserts in position

dividers at a level approximately 1in (25mm) below the upper entrances. The 'walls' of the upper compartments should fill the roof void to the apex, although a gap of one or two inches is not significant.

Wood Treatment/Final Painting

Treat the internal surfaces thoroughly with a clear preservative such as Solignum or Cuprinol.

The exterior should be white-painted using either an opaque white wood treatment such as Sadolin Pinotex Superdec (which I use), or some other microporous painting system. Try to avoid using traditional oil-based paint systems which will crack and blister rather too quickly. One of the drawbacks in using a non-gloss treatment is that it is not easy to remove dirty marks, so be careful during handling and final installation.

After painting you may consider screwing a brass cupboard knob, or some other embellishment such as a turned wood finial, onto the roof apex.

The Post

Plane the 12ft (3.6m) length of 4×4in (100×100mm) tanalised timber to remove the worst of any surface irregularities. Chamfer the edges using a circular saw (set at 45°) or plane. The chamfer should be broad to reflect the octagonal shape of the dovecote. The last 39in (1m) of the post will be set into the ground, so no preparation is needed.

Plane the 2×2in (50×50mm) tanalised timber and cut four brackets with a maximum dimension of 22in (550mm) and ends angled at 60° and 30° respectively, to form bracket supports between dovecote and post (see p.107).

Pre-drill two holes, at an angle, through the top of the post to accept 3in (75mm) no 10/12 zinc screws driven through into the dovecote base. Pre-drill further holes through the end of brackets to accept screws driven into dovecote base and post.

Stain and treat post and brackets with a product such as Sadolin Classic (PX65) Walnut.

Installation

Select a site sympathetic to the overall garden plan, ensuring that at least 20ft (6m) of open space is available 270° around the dovecote. Do not position under trees such as lime, which will drop sap.

Dig a hole about 18in (450mm) square and 39in (1m)

deep, being careful to save good turf and topsoil for reinstatement.

Bring the dovecote close to the site and lay it on its side, on a blanket or other protective surface, so that the base battens are vertical and the base is at 90° to the ground. Locate the centre of the base and hold the post, with two screws inserted into pre-drilled holes, against the base. Use a wheelbarrow or garden bench to support the post at precisely 90° to the base of the dovecote and in the central position. Drive in the two screws.

Check the angle of post to base (90°) and fix brackets in turn round the base (30° angle to dovecote base). Once these brackets are secured the dovecote may be lifted using the post and brackets only, and care should be taken not to touch the white dovecote during installation.

With assistance, raise the dovecote into the prepared hole and satisfy yourself as to position, height etc. Using a spirit level and four pieces of strong timber (3 to 5ft (1–1.5m) long) support the dovecote in the correct position (nail the timber temporarily to the post and push ends firmly into the ground).

Mix a wheelbarrow full of concrete (5 or 6 parts ballast to 1 part ordinary cement) and work this round the base of the post with a spade or baulk of timber. Fill remaining hole with earth and firm down; re-lay turf round the base.

INTRODUCING DOVES

New populations of doves need to be confined within the dovecote for at least three weeks. The most satisfactory way of doing this is to drape a strawberry net over the dovecote and down to the ground to provide a funnel of enclosed space large enough to allow them to fly from two compartments down to the ground. In this way the doves may be fed and watered conveniently during captivity; after three weeks they should regard their new surroundings as home and the net may be removed. They will usually fly away for a few hours, or perhaps even a day or so, before returning to take up permanent residence.

I suggest that a new population should be started with two breeding pairs purchased from a commercial breeder, and preferably one many miles away. A lot of local pet shops have made a lot of money selling the same pair of doves over and over again, so *beware*. Neither should you accept doves from your neighbour down the road, as they are unlikely to stay.

CARE AND MAINTENANCE

The dovecote should be mucked out once a year unless you observe problems such as maggots, dead birds etc, in which case the dovecote should be cleaned out immediately and disinfected thoroughly. Breeding pairs will use the same nest mound (made from sticks and mud) to rear as many as three broods (one or two young each time) each year.

The flat surfaces should be painted regularly and the whole dovecote redecorated as required.

9 Wall-mounted dovecotes

The Cottage dovecote may be very easily adapted for wall mounting, in a variety of configurations – six-sided, four-sided and two-sided. The advantage of wall mounting is most obvious where there is a restricted garden area, or in town houses. The six-sided dovecote, which goes round a corner wall, can be used very successfully as an architectural feature, giving relief to a plain wall in much the same way as an oriel window.

Fig 1 Six-sided dovecote mounted on corner

Six-sided 'round the corner' dovecote

Fig 1 shows a six-sided dovecote mounted on a corner wall. Fig 2 gives plan and elevation views of the structure, showing essential design and fixings. (Fig 1 shows an upright support, as the shelf precluded the use of brackets.) The points of design that differ from the free-standing construction are as follows:

Base Construct a threequarter base using additional lengths of batten to reinforce the 'corner' edges. Try to assess the position of supporting brackets in final installation and secure base battens in such a way that the intended bracket positions are not compromised.

Compartment dividers Construct walls and threequarter floor as described in the main project and use walls to 'tie-in' the open back of the dovecote and create a rigid structure.

Supports Ideally a timber support system such as that shown in Fig 2 should be used. This comprises a 24in (600mm) length of 4×4in (100×100mm) tanalised timber with a 90° section cut from its length so that it will fit flush round the corner (Fig 2). This support should be Rawl-bolted to the wall and the dovecote mounted on it and secured with further bolts, inserted through brass shelf brackets, into the wall (Fig 2).

With the dovecote in place two additional timber braces made from 2×2in (50×50mm) tanalised timber should be positioned (Fig 2). Nominally these supports should be 22in (550mm) in their longest dimension and cut at 30° to the dovecote base and 60° to the supporting post. Secure with 2½in (63mm) no 10 zinc-plated screws.

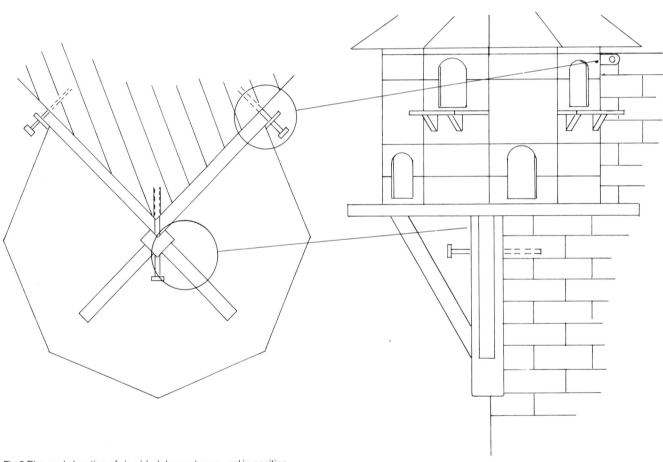

Fig 2 Plan and elevation of six-sided dovecote secured in position

Four-sided 'On The Wall' Dovecote

Fig 3 shows a four-sided dovecote in position. In this example I have made the half-dovecote in such a way that it has three full-width sides and two half-width sides, providing three nesting boxes, so that the entrances are visually balanced round the structure. Normally the dovecote would be of four equal sides with four entrances and compartments. The essential points of design for a *four*-sided dovecote are as follows:

Base The base comprises half of the octagonal base, with supporting battens at 90° to the 'back' (Fig 3), and the base tongue and groove running 'across' the structure. This configuration allows supporting brackets to seat conveniently against the base, alongside the supporting battens (Fig 3). Fig 4 shows the structure nearing completion.

Fig 4 Four-sided dovecote nearing completion

Fig 3 Four-sided dovecote in position

Compartment dividers Sections of exterior ply to divide the upper and lower spaces into compartments will need to be pinned or slotted into position as shown in Fig 5. The half-floor should be supported by pieces of batten screwed to the inside of wall sections (Fig 5). The whole should be finished with a single section of exterior ply across the back, screwed to the floor, wall and roof frames. This will provide the structure with additional rigidity.

Supports Two angle brackets made from 2×2in (50× 50mm) tanalised timber should be Rawl-bolted to the wall to provide firm and permanent support for the dovecote. Fig 3 shows these brackets clearly. With brackets in place, mount the dovecote so that it may be secured to the brackets with zinc-plated screws driven *up* through the brackets into the dovecote base. In the picture you may notice some screws protruding from base battens. These screws are used to keep the dovecote base clear of the trailer floor during transport.

Two-sided 'In The Corner' Dovecote

The two-sided version is simply one quarter of the octagonal structure, with exterior ply floor and sides. It may be hung or bolted to a wall or fence as required.

Finish

If a dovecote is to be installed against a white wall it is perhaps worthwhile providing a colour contrast by highlighting some part of the structure with, for example, gold enamel paints.

Parts of the dovecote that benefit from the addition of some form of colour highlighting are the trimming pieces on roofs, and the edges and undersides of roofs and ledges. It is not advisable to apply too much colour to areas that will be made dirty by the birds; coloured areas will become more *obviously* dirty, more quickly, than white.

Fig 5 Plywood inserts for four-sided dovecote

10 Gate

The critical factors in the design of a gate are the strength and stability of the supporting post, and the lateral strength and rigidity of the gate structure itself. The lateral strength of a conventional gate derives from the positioning of diagonal bars within the structure, bracing the 'framework' bars so that a rigid 'box' is formed. This project uses the same device, but in a more obvious and simplified way, and as a feature of design. The vertical hinge post of the gate extends to join with an exaggerated diagonal spar connecting the three horizontal bars.

A skid has been fitted to the bottom of the gate at the latch end

It should be noted that the diagonal of a gate normally runs from the bottom hinged corner to the top, thus lifting the 'toe' of the gate. As regards this sort of support, this project places the emphasis firstly on the gate being in contact with the ground in its closed position, and secondly on the use of a metal skid to restrict the potential for downwards movement of the gate during opening. This particular gate is both light and strong, and in a very public position, and has so far survived at least twenty movements per day. Should you wish, however, to make the gate even more rigid, then the installation of a second diagonal spar, running contrary to the first, is suggested.

The design and materials' specifications are suitable for spans of up to about 11ft (3.3m). The open style of the gate makes it unsuitable for keeping in small animals unless modified with the addition of vertical bars or plastic-coated mesh laid across the structure. However well made a gate is, it will inevitably suffer from being 'swung on' – the metal 'skid' on the opening side should prevent the 'toe' dropping, and relieve pressure on the gate timber and hinges.

It is important to select very straight, well dried lengths of joinery timber for this project. It may not be possible to obtain tanalised timber conforming to this standard, as the tanalising process can often warp timber to a degree. Vacuum treatment with clear preservative is less stressful to the wood and may be a realistic option. You should talk about this with the woodyard staff before ordering specific lengths. At the end of the day you may choose to buy untreated timber that you know to be straight, and rely on Sadolin, or a similar wood treatment, for protection. If this choice is made then you must ensure that all 'hidden' surfaces are treated during construction.

MATERIALS

Gate timber: 4×2in (100×50mm) tanalised or vacuum-treated planed (PSE) joinery softwood
2×2in (50×50mm) PSE softwood for gate jamb
½in (12.5mm) hardwood dowel (for dowel joints if required)
Posts: 4×4in (100×100mm) or larger tanalised post
Fixings: Galvanised bolts/washers (unless dowel used)
    Zinc-plated screws
    'Strap' hinges or similar, with bolts/screws
    Ballast and cement for 4:1 concrete mix
Treatment: Opaque white wood treatment or spirit-based coloured wood treatment.

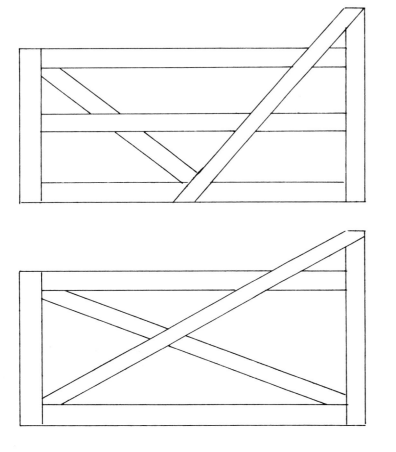
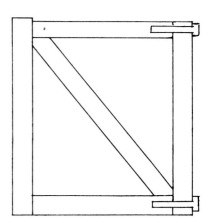

Fig 1 Alternative forms of construction

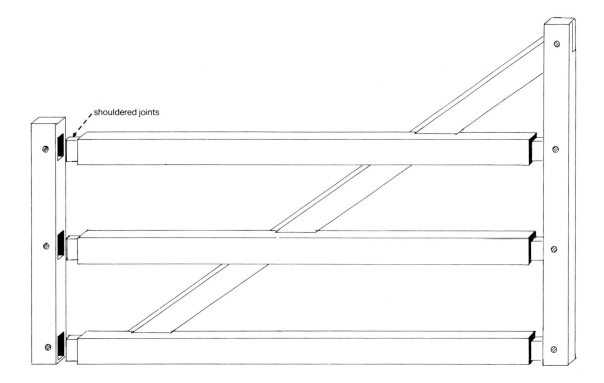

shouldered joints

Construction

Fig 2 Sectional construction of gate

Fig 2 shows the component parts of the illustrated gate, with three horizontal bars jointed into two pillars, one of which is extended to join with an exaggerated diagonal spar.

Having decided on the height of the gate and thus the required height of pillars, cut two lengths of 4×2in (100× 50mm) planed joinery timber to the appropriate length. The illustrated gate is 39in (1m) high (bar to bar) and the supporting pillar is 59in (1.5m) long. In general, the wider the gate, the higher the pillar should be. A 6ft (1.8m) gate, 39in (1m) high, should have a pillar approximately 51in (1.3m) long.

Clamp the prepared timbers together, with ends flush, and measure and mark the positions for three mortice joints. These joints should be 3in (75mm) deep by 1in (25mm) wide and 4in (100mm) (nominal) long. The bottom joints may be 'open' to the end of pillars.

Using a 1in (25mm) flat wood bit, drill out mortices, being careful that the lead point of the drill bit does not protrude through the wrong side of the timber. Finish mortices with a sharp chisel and square off. Advice on the preparation of mortice and tenon joints may be found in the Oak Bench (p.85) and the Footbridge (p.72) projects.

Tenons should be shouldered (see other projects) and taken right through object timber for strength and rigidity. It is also a good idea to wedge the joints tight with galvanised steel wedges driven into tenon ends (as one would do if fixing a new head to an axe or mallet).

Prepare three identical horizontal bars: clamp together to mark 3in (75mm) tenon joints on both ends of each; define the extent of tenons with a tenon saw; and saw, chisel or plane these tenons to provide a tight, flush fit into mortices. Repeatedly 'test' joints during preparation and ensure that the 'shoulders' of the tenons fit tightly and evenly against the morticed timber.

With all tenon joints prepared apply waterproof wood glue to the tenons and join pillars and bars. Ensure that the gate is 'square', using a 90° set square, before starting to fix joints with dowels or bolts.

Use either dowels or bolts to secure joints – on balance I should say that bolts should be preferred, galvanised if possible. Instructions for dowelling may be found in the Footbridge and Oak Bench projects (pp.72 and 85) and you should be particularly careful not to damage the wood by allowing flat wood bits to 'exit' from the 'wrong side' or by over-enthusiastic insertion of dowels. If using bolts this should be in conjunction with large flat-washers on both faces.

If 'strap' hinges are to be used these should be aligned so that the first bolt hole on the strap is over the mortice/tenon joint of a bar. The bolt for this joint should go through both the strap and the joint. The use of iron strap hinges should be preferred in this project rather than the 'parliament' hinges illustrated. I just happened to have these available at the time. With structure secured and checked for squareness, lay the diagonal spar across the horizontal bars and mark it at each cross-over point with bars and pillar. Cut ½–¾in (12–18mm) joints from the diagonal spar so that it will joint-in with the bars; there should also be a cut-away at the top of the long pillar to keep all in line. Glue and bolt (or screw) the diagonal bar to the gate timbers at all cross-over points.

Gate Posts/Hinges

It is extremely important to secure gate posts permanently and immovably. This requires the creation of a substantial concrete foundation. A gate post set into a normal earth base (land that has not been already surfaced with concrete or a road surface) should be inserted into a hole at least 24in (600mm) deep and 18in (450mm) square, packed with at least 16in (400mm) of strong concrete (4 parts ballast to 1 part ordinary cement). Unless the gate post is to be connected with a strong fence, an additional diagonal support should be jointed into the post and concreted into the ground (see Fig 3).

The 'hinge' post should be continued for some inches above the level of the top horizontal bar to accommodate the 'strap' hinges, if these are used. (If cut flush with the top bar there will not be enough room to secure hinges to the gate post.)

If possible install the 'bearing' post and hinge the gate to it *before* fixing the 'closing' post. In this way you will be able to fit and secure the closing post very accurately.

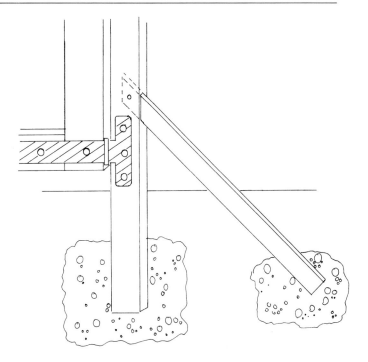

Fig 3 Concrete gate-post foundations

When in final position secure a length of 2×2in (50× 50mm) timber as a jamb and fit an appropriate gate latch.

If required make a skid from a length of galvanised steel shaped around the bottom of the gate. Secure with galvanised nails or screws.

11 Revolving summerhouse

This is a difficult and interesting construction and you will need to keep your wits about you at all times during preparation and construction. It is not a project for the faint-hearted but if you treat it as a challenge, and are successful, then you will have a beautiful and interesting piece of garden architecture (and a lot of new skills) to show for it.

It has not been possible to include every tiny piece of information that may be needed, as that would require a book in itself. I have had to assume that anybody taking on this project is already versed in simple woodwork technique. If you doubt your ability to build the summerhouse my suggestion would be for you to build a dovecote first. Most of the necessary construction principles are to be found in that project, albeit on a smaller scale, and mistakes will be a lot less expensive.

In this project, more than any other, think *twice*, measure *twice*, cut *once* – and check that that cut is right *before* you cut any more.

The summerhouse illustrated has a maximum floor span (point to point) of 11ft (3.2m), which makes it a substantial structure with room enough inside to seat four or five people round a table. The size that you choose to construct will depend on the intended use and the site chosen so, throughout the project, it is left to you to provide precise dimensions.

There may be aspects of design that you wish to change or develop. If so, it must be remembered that the revolving summerhouse is an integrated system with each component relying on another for structural integrity. Any substitutions or changes in design must take this into account.

Before you start constructing, it may be as well quickly to consider the basic order of procedure:

1 Read the project thoroughly, including sections referred to in Chapter 3 General Construction Principles (GCP) p.47.
2 Decide on the dimensions and shape of your summerhouse and draw a plan with these marked on it. Refer to Chapter 3, Multi-facet Structures p.47 and establish all the relevant angles (roof pitch, roof section apex, frame angles etc). Decide on the size and style of door you require and the sizes that will fit your plan.
3 Decide on the thickness of timber you will use for door frames and, with this in mind, see your local engineers and order all the metal parts needed for the project. These are identified and illustrated in the project (see materials' list for Fig nos).
4 Work out your timber requirements, with reference to the materials' list, and order.
5 When the metal parts are ready paint them all with Hammerite, Steelcote or bituminous paint. Do not leave this until final assembly.
6 Commence construction.

MATERIALS

Foundations: 4 parts to 1 part mix of ballast and ordinary cement (reinforced with old iron, steel or wire)
Pivot, wheels and steel supports: As described in text and in Figs 1, 2, 5, 7, – 10. For these parts you should take the book, and show the relevant sections and diagrams to your local fabricating engineer. He will be able to produce the parts to order
Base frame: Lengths of 4×2in (100×50mm) tanalised (sawn) softwood
Floor: 1×5in (25×125mm) tongue and groove PSE (planed square edge) softwood plank (tanalised)
Wall and roof frames: Minimum 2×1in (50×25mm) PSE softwood
Wall cladding: 1×5in (25×125mm) shiplap; or tongue and groove, V or matching
Roof cladding: ¾×5in (19×125mm) shiplap
Flashing: Mineral felt and mastic
Fixings: Galvanised nails, zinc-plated screws etc
Electrical: Armoured cable and electrical equipment as described in text
Doors: As required

SPECIAL TOOLS

Circular saw with angle facility
Hand-held electric plane
Hand-held jig-saw

Construction

Constructing a level foundation: The revolving mechanism of the summerhouse is very simple, involving a single, central, circular steel pivot (Fig 1a) and eight nylon wheels, revolving on a bed of concrete – the component parts of the mechanism may be seen in Fig 1. Load is born evenly by the nylon wheels and, by transference through the floor frame, the central pivot. To ensure structural rigidity and ease of movement, it is essential to provide a level track for the wheels.

Firstly decide on the diameter of the structure. One factor to take into account will be door size and configuration, as external panel size (the maximum door-frame aperture) will reduce in proportion to any reduction in overall diameter.

Using a piece of *non-elastic* string and large nails or screw drivers mark the centre point of your site and gouge a line around the circumference of your chosen circle.

At the centre point dig a hole 20in (500mm) in diameter by 16in (400mm) deep. Fill this hole with a strong mix of concrete (4 to 1) and insert the *female* pivot (Fig 2) in such a way that, when the male is inserted, the distance from the

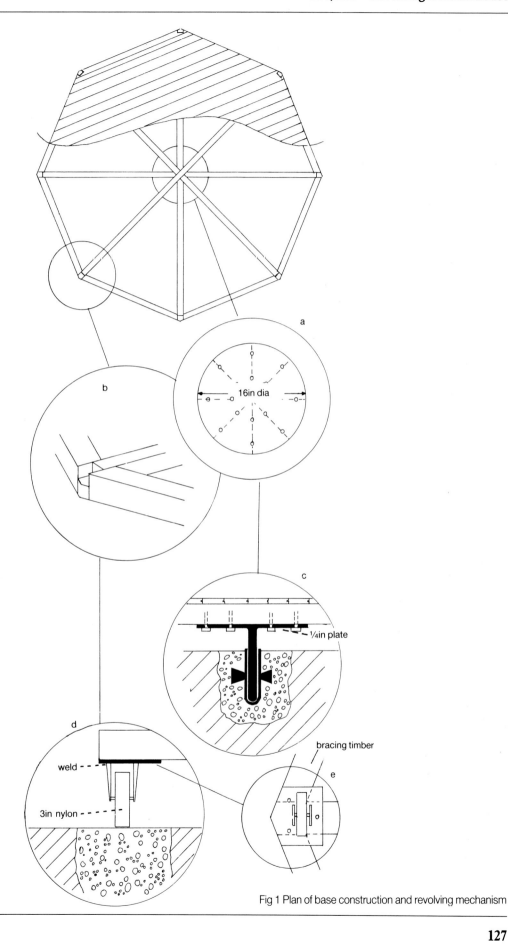

a

16in dia

b

c

¼in plate

d

weld

3in nylon

bracing timber

e

Fig 1 Plan of base construction and revolving mechanism

Fig 2 'Female' bearing in position – set in concrete foundation

Fig 3 Completed summerhouse foundation

ground to the top of the male pivot plate is equal to the distance from the projected *wheel* base to the top of the *wheel* mounting. Ensure that the female pivot is vertical and protect it from the rain. (To ensure a vertical fit, position the male pivot in the female and use a spirit level on pivot base plate (Fig 1c).)

Dig a trench at least 8in (200mm) wide and 10in (250mm) deep around the circumference of the circle so that the wheels will move *centrally* on the concrete foundation. Bear in mind that the wheels will not be sited at the extreme of the summerhouse dimension, but 1–2in (25–50mm) in towards the centre, depending on their type and the plates to which they are welded (Fig 1a). Check this aspect before you commence. They need to be placed as far *in* as possible, so as to minimise the risk of persons (especially children) getting their feet in the path of the wheels.

Select a length of 2×4in (50×100mm) sawn tanalised timber (floor frame) and cut it to just over the required maximum diameter. Position and secure the male pivot with coach screws, so that it is in an exactly central position on the timber length (Fig 1c). The timber should, of course, present its narrow side to the metal plate. (Remember, the metal pivot parts and wheel assemblies should have been painted, prior to use, with Steelcote, Hammerite or a bituminous protective finish to inhibit rust.)

Temporarily secure a wheel at each end of the timber in the position they will eventually adopt.

When the central pivot concrete is set (24 hours), position the male pivot so that you are able to spin the assembly round. (Lubricate the female pivot with a liberal application of heavy duty grease.) Start filling the prepared trench with concrete (4 to 1) reinforcing it with any old

iron, steel or wire that you may have lying around. As you fill the trench you will be able to assess the correct level by reference to the wheel positions and a spirit level laid along the timber. You should end up with a concrete foundation on which the wheels can revolve freely and evenly. At this point remove the wheel assembly and trowel the concrete surface smooth. Protect the finished concrete from rain and frost (see Fig 3 for completed foundation).

Electrical installation: If you intend to supply electricity to the summerhouse you should lay ARMOURED CABLE underneath the foundation so that at least 13ft (4m) lies within the circle described by the concrete. (See Fig 5). To assess the grade of cable you need, describe the services that you will require to your supplier and let him tell you what you should use (later paragraphs deal further with electrical installation, p.129).

Base frame construction: The summerhouse base frame is made of lengths of 2×4in (50×100mm) tanalised sawn timber, bolted to the central pivot plate and wheel mountings. Fig 1 clearly shows the significant construction principles.

Cut two lengths of timber to span the required diameter, so that each end comes to a point with a cut of 22½° on either side (Fig 1b). Joint these timbers with a halving joint so that they can cross each other at their centre points. With reference to the finished thickness of the wall frame timbers (Fig 4b) saw and chisel out a joint (of 2in (50mm) depth) at each end of the base frame timbers (Fig 1b). Using coach screws, in pre-drilled holes, secure the two timbers to the central pivot plate at *exactly* 90° to each other. 88° will not be good enough!

Now prepare and secure four lengths of timber so that their ends are precisely the same distance from the centre

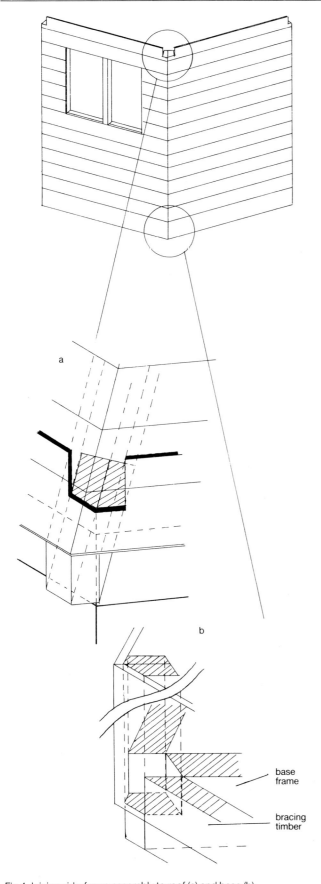

a

b

base
frame

bracing
timber

Fig 4 Joining side-frame assembly to roof (a) and base (b)

of the frame as the four already prepared. There is no room for error at this stage. (Note: Fig 11 shows one of the base-frame timbers extended beyond the octagonal base to allow a particular application of door restraints. You may wish to use this feature, depending on the type of door restraint you wish to use.) These timbers should be temporarily secured with nails, to the pivot plate, at 45° to the existing pieces. With the finished eight-pointed frame lying on a level surface, measure the distance between each of the eight points (however careful you have been there is certain to be some small difference in measurement). Add these dimensions together and divide the total by eight. This will give you the measurement for the eight bracing timbers to be installed around the circumference of the octagon. Cut eight lengths of timber to this precise dimension using a 22½° angle at each cut so that the timber lies exactly flush against the frames (Fig 1b – and can just be seen in Fig 6).

Secure these timbers with 4in (100mm) galvanised nails driven through pre-drilled holes and, finally, secure wheel assemblies across each joint with coach screws (Fig 1d and e).

Install the completed floor frame (refer to Fig 1) at the site.

Electrical installation: If electricity is to be run to the summerhouse it is necessary to sacrifice complete rotational mobility and limit the movement of the summerhouse to, say, 359°. This is because there is a limit to the flexibility of the armoured cable power supply.

With reference to Fig 5, firmly drive in the angle iron stop so that its top is just below the floor frame. Secure the flat stop plate to the frame timber so that it comes against the angle iron stop at the end of a revolution. Lay the armoured cable round the central pivot and secure it to the floor frame (Fig 5) in such a way that it will not be stressed

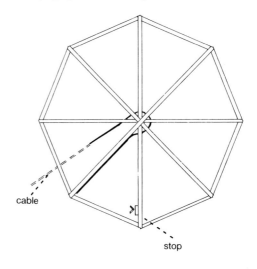

cable

stop

Fig 5 Laying armoured cable

by the summerhouse movement, nor trapped under the summerhouse wheels. When laying the floor you should bring the cable through the floor adjacent to a wall section frame, but *not* a door frame.

Laying the floor: Begin laying 1in (25mm) planed, tanalised tongue and groove boards onto the base frame. Be careful to ensure that it is laid right side up (some tongue and grooves are not located centrally in the wood and will only lie flush if assembled in one particular way). Lay the floor as in Fig 1, so that each board runs to the outside edge of the floor frame; at each point of the octagon, cut out a small piece to accommodate the wall frames, which at these points must fit into the base frame – see Fig 6, also Figs 4b and 1b. To secure the floor use 2in (50mm) narrow-head galvanised nails.

Stain the completed floor frame with a spirit-based stain or Sadolin.

Wall sections: The summerhouse illustrated has six identical wall sections seating into apertures in the base frame and bolting to one another. Door frames bridge the gaps between the first and last wall sections (Fig 13). Rigidity is achieved by bolting the sections, securing them to the base frames and by fitting the roof. Additional rigidity is provided with a number of steel reinforcements round the door frames. However, the single most important factor in achieving a strong and cohesive result, is accuracy in production. This should be borne in mind at all times.

To reproduce wall sections accurately you will need to construct templates for producing components, and a jig for final assembly. Refer to Chapter 3 General Construction Principles for this information and for production instructions (p.47).

Read GCP with reference to the completed base and be sure that you fully understand the principles involved before you start production. Fig 4 will assist you in this.

The summerhouse is clad with 1×5in (25×125mm) shiplap pine, which is quite satisfactory. A better result (for wall sections) will be achieved with 1×5in (25× 125mm) tongue and groove. As it will not be in contact with the ground the timber need not be tanalised, although this treatment is always preferable. If not tanalised it should be treated with preservative (clear if the structure is to be painted). Nails should be 2in (50mm) narrow head galvanised.

In construction of wall sections pay particular attention to the following:

1 Number frame parts and pre-drill bolt holes in frames in such a way that, when you match frame **A** to frame **B** the bolts will insert readily and accurately. You will not be able to drill and bolt successfully if you leave it till final

assembly as the angle of one panel to another will prevent the use of a drill.
2 Ensure that you reflect the chosen pitch of the roof in the top angle of each frame.
3 When you have made the first wall section *check that it fits* to the base frame before you make any more.

Dimensions It is for you to decide on a suitable wall height but, in general, this should be around 7ft (2.1m). Width of wall sections will be dictated by base dimensions.

Windows This summerhouse does not have windows. Should you wish to install one or two refer to Windows in GCP (p.53) for a simple system of construction. Window frames should be braced against wall section frames, rather than rely on cladding for sole support.

Roof section production: Before ordering materials or starting work on roof sections you will need to decide on the pitch of your roof, its materials and finish. The model in this project has a roof pitch (at frame) of 35° – giving an apex angle for each section of 36.5° and frame angle of 13.4°. The roof is of 1×5in (25×125mm) shiplap pine, treated with Sadolin Extra (see Timber Treatment p.00 for information on this product). You may choose to use V-jointed or matching tongue and groove for construction, as this can give a more weatherproof finish, provided that the roof pitch is steep enough to allow water to run away from joints. Whichever timber is used, its profile should not allow any collection of water in the joints. Satisfy yourself on this point before ordering timber.

I settled on this type of wooden roof cladding because I thought a mineral felt roof would spoil the character of the structure, and other constructions such as shingles or tiles are too heavy. The design is not ideal, as any faults either in the wood or in construction may cause seepage, unless the wood is properly waterproofed and the joints properly flashed with lead, felt or timber. If tongue and groove timber is used, and the roof is to be painted, it will help to paint the tongue and grooves and assemble them while still wet, thus providing a sealed joint. It may also be useful to use a clear silicon sealant along the section joints during assembly. One way generally to improve the roof is to raise the pitch and thus provide better drainage, but this must depend on your overall design concept.

Procedure With reference to Multi-facet Structures in GCP (p.47), establish the necessary constructional angles for your chosen pitch of roof.

By drawing an accurate model, showing the radius of the summerhouse base and the proposed pitch of roof, assess the length of roof frame sections. Allow roof to overlap walls by at least 6in (150mm); remember to take measurements at the 'points' of the shape (the longest dimension).

Using techniques already experienced in Jig 1 construct

Jig 2 (GCP p.52). This jig should be made so that timber cladding may be laid across roof frames and cut to size in-situ (as with the pergola construction). It is simpler to opt for this method when dealing with large roof structures than to attempt using a template. Produce eight identical roof sections.

Wall installation Having completed six wall sections (with or without windows), and eight roof sections, begin assembly by placing a wall section in base frame apertures (see Fig 6). Be sure that you know where you intend the doors to go, and that the summerhouse 'stop' operates at a convenient stage in the rotation (you do not want the stop to interfere with the 'normal' arc of use). Position a second wall section (in the numbered order) and bolt to the first. As each section is completed drill at an angle through the inside face of the unfinished bottom end of each wall frame and secure to the base frame timber with a 4in (100mm) zinc screw or galvanised nail. Use 2in (50mm) galvanised nails to secure the bottom cladding pieces to the bracing timbers of the base. Continue assembly until all six sections are secured in position.

Door frames/steel supports Figs 7–13 show the suggested plan and components for door-frame assembly and support. These can only be a guide, as final door-jamb thickness etc will depend on the size of door and width of door aperture that you have elected to use.

Fig 6 Position of wall sections in base

Fig 7 Plan of door components and installation

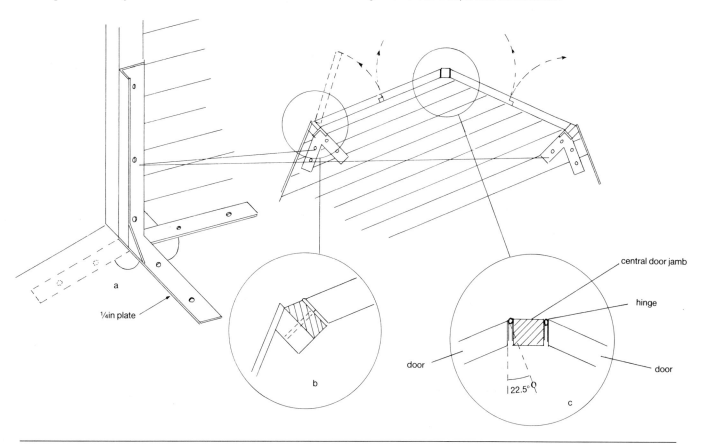

¼in plate

a

b

central door jamb

hinge

door

door

22.5°

c

Fig 8 Installation of steel reinforcement on first panel

1 You first need to prepare and fix two lengths of wall frame timber to bolster the wall supports of the first and last of the six wall sections. This timber will also act as a door frame to which hinges will be secured. This is shown in Fig 7b and Fig 10.

2 Using coach screws and bolts turned into pre-drilled holes, secure the two steel supports (Fig 8). It is essential to ensure that the door jambs are *precisely vertical* before finally securing these steel supports.

3 Prepare and fix the central door jamb (Figs 7c and 11) so that its length and top angle are precisely the same as wall section frames. Fix this jamb, with a long coach screw or heavy zinc screw, into its base frame aperture.

4 Prepare and fix two bracing timbers spanning door apertures (see Fig 13), using steel brackets as shown in Figs 9, 10 and 13. Check that door frame measurements are correct in every respect and leave gaps above and below the doors to allow them to open and close easily. Remember that they will need to open beyond the roof overhang; you will need either to provide sufficient height in the structure (or width in the top bracing timbers) to allow unimpeded opening *or* you will have to remove the lower cladding from the appropriate roof facets.

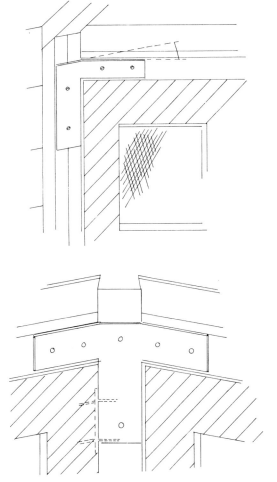

Fig 9 Steel supports for upper door frames

Fig 10 Section showing upper door frame assembly

Fig 11 Section showing lower door assembly and furniture

Fig 12 Section showing lower door frame assembly and reinforcement

Fig 13 Completed wall and door frame assembly

5 Either now or later, when the roof is in position, carefully assess door positions and plane or saw the appropriate angle (eight-sided = 22½°) from the hinge side of each door so that they will close onto their jambs (Fig 7c). Use brass hinges set into doors and jambs for door-hanging.

6 After treating or staining timber, fit door furniture as required. Fit catches onto the 'elongated' base frames to hold each door in the open position so that they are secure against the wind – see Fig 11.

7 Glaze the doors with ⅛in (4mm) glass using coloured exterior putty or wood quadrants pressed against a silicon sealant and secured with copper or brass tacks or similar.

8 Span any gap above the doors with cladding and, if necessary, provide door closures to prevent rain and draught entering around the doors.

Roof assembly If at all possible it is worthwhile assembling and finishing the roof *on the ground* (see Fig 14) and then lifting it into final position. This places less stress on the structure and allows the roof to be lowered evenly onto its supports. For the purposes of this project I will assume that this is the way you have chosen. If section by section assembly is chosen it will be important to check that each section fits its partner precisely *before* final assembly. Instruction for section-by-section assembly will be as with the pergola, see p.140.

Procedure

1 Each of the roof sections should be treated *externally* with a waterproof product such as Sadolin Extra which will properly seal the timber. Each section should be treated *internally* with a spirit-based product such as Cuprinol. Try to keep the inside colour as light as possible.

2 Join roof sections together with the panels lying upside-down on a reasonably level surface, being careful not to damage the finish. Before finally securing each joint squeeze some silicon sealant, or similar, along its *outside edge* to provide a waterproof barrier. As you add more panels provide support for the structure at all times.

3 Once all sections are bolted and sealed turn the roof over, being careful not to damage the edges.

4 Flash each joint with felt, lead or a timber moulding, backed up with a liberal application of silicon or mastic. Secure felt or lead with roofing felt 'clouts' but be very careful not to split the wood (either pre-drill or fix well away from the joints). Install a 'cap' of felt or lead to the roof apex (see Fig 14). Fig 15 shows a detail of simple felt flashing. I would also recommend the provision of shallow drainage channels (shown) which will help to divert surface water from the joints. If using either felt or lead for flashing, carry out the operation on a dry, warm day, which will make the materials rather easier to handle. Felt

Fig 14 Completed roof assembly and installation

Fig 15 Section of roof showing drainage channels and flashing

should be glued down with bituminous mastic, and lead moulded to the profile of the wood with a rubber hammer or a combination of wood batten and steel hammer. Steel hammers should not come into direct contact with the lead. Wood mouldings should be secured with narrow galvanised nails inserted at 90° to the moulded faces; they should be generously pre-drilled so that no pressure is applied to the moulding during insertion of nails – they have an annoying tendency to split easily. For all this work you will be able to lie across the roof, preferably using a plank or ladder to spread the load.

Roof installation: You will need *at least* three assistants for this operation. Do not attempt it with less as the roof will be very heavy, and its installation awkward.

Procedure
1 Secure the summerhouse so that it cannot rotate.
2 Lift the roof, by the frames only, and lean it against the summerhouse at a steep angle, ready for lifting into position. Do not lean it against the doors or door frames.
3 With two step-ladders, and one assistant inside the summerhouse lift the roof up and over the structure. Try not to put any pressure on the summerhouse walls and use lengths of sturdy timber (against joints) to help position roof. Once the roof is balanced on the summerhouse move yourself and assistants inside to lift roof into its final position.

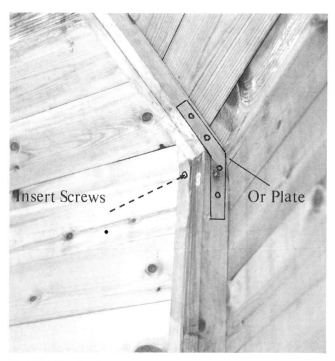

Insert Screws

Or Plate

Fig 16 Wall/roof jointing

4 When happy with the position, secure each frame with no 10 zinc screws inserted through the top of wall frame and/or with steel angle brackets as shown in Fig 16.
5 Have a cup of tea and pat yourself on the back!

Final electrical installation: Final wiring should be carried out by a competent electrician as it will require connecting into your domestic power supply.

The finished circuit should look like this: DOMESTIC FUSED SUPPLY *through* ARMOURED CABLE *to* 30 MILLIAMP FUSE BOX with ON/OFF SWITCH *through* HEAVY DUTY CABLE *to* FUSED SOCKETS and LIGHTING.

TURNING THE SUMMERHOUSE

Make up a rope handle, secured through the base frame, as a means of *pulling* the summerhouse round. *Never* try to push the structure round by leaning against walls or door frames.

Always check that there are no obstructions in the path of the wheels before turning the summerhouse. This is *particularly* important in relation to the fingers and feet of small children, who should always be kept well clear of the summerhouse during turning.

---

12 Pergola

Visitors to Mediterranean countries will be accustomed to having lunch or drinks on a veranda covered with a slatted roof. In hot countries this structure offers some protection from the sun while still providing a light, warm area in which to sit.

The role of the pergola in an English country garden is twofold. On a hot summer's day it provides a shaded spot in the garden; and through the rest of the year, it provides an unsurpassed vehicle for climbing plants such as clematis, honeysuckle and rose. In a landscaped garden with long walks and secret corners the pergola may be used for design purposes, perhaps in conjunction with an arboured walkway or pathways hedged with the same plants that climb the pergola.

Securing roof sections in situ

The structure illustrated was built for a garden centre as a way to encourage customers into a rather neglected corner. I look forward to the day when I will be able to take my family for lunch to a landscaped pub garden, complete with pergolas and climbing plants, rather than with plastic tables and a worn-out lawn.

The pergola illustrated is essentially octagonal, although four sides are short and four long. It covers an area 13ft 4in (4m) in diameter. To make a smaller structure you simply need to scale down the materials and measurements – the construction techniques (angles etc) remain constant. You may wish to paint all or part of your pergola and this may mean buying different materials, as tanalised timber will not always accept some oil-based paints. Check with the timber-yard, and refer to Chapter 3 p.55 on this subject.

MATERIALS

Supporting posts: 3×3in (75×75mm), eight 10ft (3m) lengths, tanalised, sawn. (If the pergola is in a particularly windy area, or likely to be subjected to abnormal stresses, then upgrade these posts to 4×4in (100×100mm))

Roof section frames: 4×1in (100×25mm) PSE tanalised, 194ft (65m), but order as twelve 16ft (5.4m) lengths to avoid waste

Roof slats (battens): 1½×¾in (38×19mm) PSE tanalised, 1000ft (300m)

Seats: 3×2in (75×50mm) PSE tanalised, 60ft (18m)
1½×1½in (38×38mm) PSE tanalised *unless* seats are to be painted (see note above), 100ft (30m)

Trellis: ½×1½in (13×38mm) PSE tanalised, as required

Fixings:

Bolts for roof sections: Twenty-four 2½×¼in (63×6mm) galvanised bolts plus forty-eight washers

Screws for roof sections: Eighty 1½in (38mm) no 10 zinc-plated
Eighty 3in (75mm) no 10 zinc-plated (4in (100mm) if posts are upgraded to 4×4in (100×100mm))

Screws for seats: Thirty-four 3in (75mm) no 10 zinc-plated
Forty-two 2½in (63mm) no 10 zinc-plated

Nails: 2lb (1kg) of 1½in (38mm) narrow galvanised nails
1lb (½kg) of 1in (25mm) narrow galvanized nails

Sand, cement, stain, etc: as required

SPECIAL TOOLS

Normal workshop tools, plus
Electric plane
Circular saw with angle attachment
Two G clamps (4in (100mm) min)

Construction

Preparation of timber posts: Using a circular saw or plane, chamfer the corners of each of the eight supporting posts and plane smooth so that, if viewed from the end, each has the profile illustrated in Figs 1, and 1a – ie an octagon with four long and four short sides. This shape mirrors the overall design of the pergola. Each post should be planed to the point where you may run your hand along the wood without picking up splinters, but you are not making a cabinet so don't overdo it. The last 32in (800mm) of each post will be buried in the ground, so this part should not be prepared in any way.

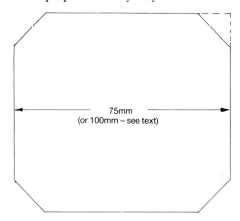

Fig 1 Section through supporting post

75mm
(or 100mm – see text)

Fig 1a Using a circular saw to prepare posts

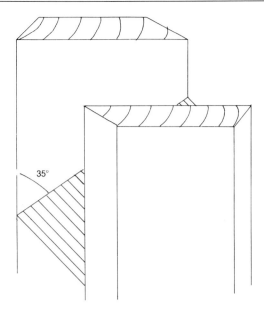

Fig 2 Section through top of post showing seat for roof frame

Fig 2a Chiseling out the seat for a roof frame

Cut a section from the top of each post, as described in Fig 2, and 2a. The width of cut should be twice the width of the timber obtained for the roof section frames (nominally 4×1in (100×25mm)). Make sure that you provide an easy fitting. (Note that with 3×3in (75×75mm) posts, this 'easy fit' for roof frames – each 1in (25mm) in thickness – will leave a bare ½in (12mm) on each side of joint; in ordinary application this construction, with proper securing, is adequate but if you are at all doubtful it

might be advisable to use 4×4in (100×100mm) tanalised timber.)

The 35° angle of cut is critical as it reflects the pitch of the roof, and the joint should be cut deep enough to provide a secure fixing through roof section frames. To assist in making the angle draw a 35° template on paper and lay each post on it in such a way that you can mark, on either side of the post, where the cut should come. An ordinary tenon saw and a chisel should be used for cutting and cleaning these apertures, into which the roof section frames will eventually seat.

Although you may wait until the posts are erected it is a good idea to stain them with a colour of your choice at this stage. Tanalised posts need no further protection against rot although you may find it convenient to apply colour in the form of a product such as Sadolin. For the pergola in this project I used Sadolin, Walnut.

Positioning of posts: Ensure that the site chosen for the pergola is level – remember that it will cover an area 13ft 4in (4m) in diameter. Do not worry too much about surface composition as you may introduce chippings, concrete or whatever surface you wish at a later stage. Decide on its centre point and push in a 6in (150mm) nail or screwdriver to mark it – tie on a 7ft (2m+) length of non-elastic string and on this string measure off 78in (2m) (secure another nail or screwdriver at this point). Now gouge out a complete circle, with your string as its 78in (2m) radius. With reference to Fig 3 use lengths of timber and string to describe four equilateral triangles, so that one point of each triangle meets at the centre of the circle. The other two points of each triangle, where they meet the circumference of the circle, will be *post positions*. Having described the four equilateral triangles and thus established the post positions, *check* that the spacing between these positions is as described in Fig 3: n = short side, 2n = long side.

The critical thing here is not that the posts are exactly 78in (2m) from the centre, but rather that they are correctly spaced in relation to one another. Check and re-check your measurements before committing the posts to concrete.

Dig neat post holes, as narrow as possible and at least 32in (800mm) deep, at each of the defined post positions. Position each post in a bed of concrete or tightly compacted soil (depending on soil structure), ensuring that the posts are exactly level with each other, and exactly vertical; also make sure that the measurements between posts are identical top and bottom. Insert posts with the angled top sections pointing *up* to the centre of the circle. Support posts with battens of wood and constantly check levels and spacings in relation to other posts.

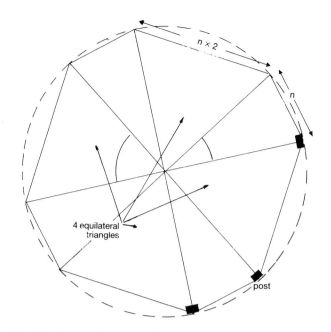

Fig 3 Plan for identifying post positions

In some circumstances (including the pergola in his project) it is possible to use metal post supports. On the whole, this is not to be recommended as they do not, in themselves, provide sufficient rigidity, they are expensive and can be difficult to position exactly.

Roof construction: The pergola roof is made in eight triangular sections, of two sizes, which bolt together and seat into the angled grooves already prepared in the eight supporting posts.

Fig 4 Completed roof section in jig

To construct these sections accurately you will first need to manufacture a jig for each size. Refer to Chapter 3 General Construction Principles p.47 for guidance in preparing and using jigs.

Each triangular section is made of lengths of ¾×1½in (19×38mm) tanalised batten nailed onto a framework of 4×1in (100×25mm) tanalised timber. The method of construction may be seen in Fig 4, which shows a finished narrow section sitting in the jig – refer to General Construction Principles (GCP) p.47, to prepare this jig which will provide the appropriate angle for a narrow roof section. Cut two pieces of 1×4in (25×100mm) timber each 9ft (2.7m) in length, and remove a 35° wedge from each end (Fig 5) so that both top and bottom will provide vertical faces when raised to roof pitch. With reference to GCP p.57 use a circular saw or plane to create the appropriate angle along each length so that, when placed in the jig, they are ready to accept battens (slats).

If you choose to leave the roof slats unstained, then you may wish to stain the frames to provide contrast. If so, this should be done now, prior to batten (slat) fixing. If you wish to stain the whole structure this should be done prior to final assembly. For information on which stains or wood treatments you may use, see GCP p.47.

Lay the prepared frames in the jig and match the apex precisely. Pre-drill and screw together using a 1½in (38mm) no 8 zinc. This will serve to hold the frame together during construction and assembly. If there is any uncertainty in the way the frames seat into the jig it is a good idea to screw them down (to the jig). If you do, make sure that you will be able to remove the screws easily when you need to.

Having established the frames in the jig, begin positioning lengths of batten (slats) starting at the bottom (widest point) and working towards the apex. Allow a ¾–1in (19–25mm) gap at the bottom before you lay on the first batten. Secure each end of each batten with a single 1½in (38mm) narrow galvanised nail and be careful to angle the nail to match the frame angle. To ensure even spacing, use a length of batten as a spacer, and cut the ends of each batten to match the angled frame as you go along (Fig 4). Also, remember to remove any securing screws, or at least leave a gap which will allow you to remove them later.

Either at this stage or later, when all sections are finished, fix fascia boards to the roof sections (see Fig 5). These are lengths of 1×4in (25×100mm) timber, each secured with four 1½in (38mm) no 8 zinc screws – to obtain a flush fitting for these boards you must saw or plane the angle revealed at the bottom of the frames (to see what this entails simply hold a length of timber to the bottom of a frame). If you have a router or jig-saw you may choose to embellish the fascia with a pattern.

Having satisfied yourself with the first roof section

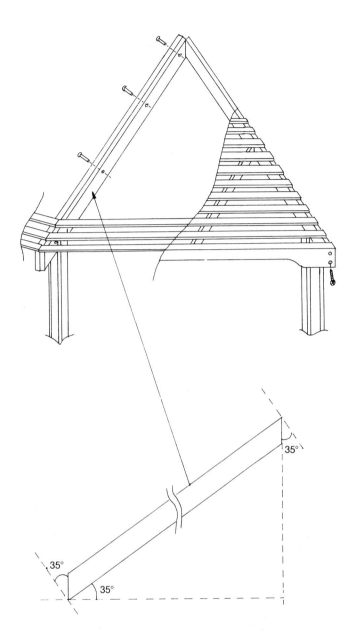

Fig 5 Exploded view of roof section construction

construction, go on to produce three more narrow sections and then re-jig for the larger panels. Precisely the same principles apply, but you will need to provide support for the slats in the lower half of each large section. One option is to provide an inverted V of additional support (Fig 5), using battens screwed through frame and fascia, to which roof slats are nailed. Do not leave spans of more than 39in (1m) without additional support. Alternatively you may choose supporting battens which run centrally *up* each wide section.

Apex Ornamentation You may wish to provide a 'dolly' or some other ornamentation for the apex of the pergola roof. If so it, or its support, should include a section 2¼–2¾in (60–70mm) square and 6in (150mm) long which will fit into the apex aperture (an approximately square hole is left in the apex of the roof once all roof sections have been joined); it can be secured with wedges of timber to make a tight, flush fit. You should fit this ornamentation before the last roof section goes into place – otherwise you will need to climb on the roof!

Roof assembly: When assembling the roof you have two choices: either, join section to section in situ; or, assemble roof on the ground and lift into position complete.

If you are able to gather at least six strong people, complete with step ladders, then option two is preferable. For option one you will need one assistant with occasional help from a second – whichever way you choose, the rules are the same. For the purposes of the book I will assume that you have chosen the first option.

Starting with a wide section raise it up so that its frame seats into the supporting posts. In the first instance the posts should be about 10in (250mm) from the fascia boards, although you will be adjusting this spacing later. To assist in raising this, and other sections, your assistant should, with the aid of a long length of timber, hold the apex at its correct height. At all times be careful not to push against unsupported spans of batten.

Once the first section is in position, and with the assistant still holding it steady with his long pole, raise a second (narrow) section. Marry this up precisely with the first and clamp the two together. After checking for precise alignment drill three bolt holes through the frames at even spacings (Fig 5). Do not drill close to the post positions as you may find, in the final adjustments, that these will have to be re-sited. Firmly secure bolts, with washers either side – Fig 6 shows how assembly should progress. At this stage you may hold the frames into the post apertures *temporarily*, using nails, but *do not* fix permanently until later.

Continue positioning roof sections, being careful to provide support at all times (either that of your assistant, or with long poles), and aim to install a *narrow* section last.

Fig 6 Finished post/roof section construction

To clamp and bolt the last section in you will need a fair amount of help. The trick is to raise the roof apex to allow the bottom of the last section to move towards its partner – be very careful not to put undue pressure on the post apertures at this stage.

Once the roof is completely assembled use a block of wood and a hammer to ensure that the posts are positioned evenly in relation to the roof frames, and that the whole structure is vertical. Once you are satisfied with the positioning, secure through the post apertures and frames with 3in (75mm) no 10 zinc screws (Fig 6).

If you have not already done so stain the fascia boards to match roof frames and supporting posts.

Seating: The pergola for this project includes a simple bench seat spanning one long, and two short, sides. Construction of this seat may be seen in Figs 7 and 8.

This construction is suggested for applications where the supporting posts are concreted in and the structure is not subject to unusual stresses. The seats rely on the integrity of the supporting posts. An alternative would be to transfer the loading to the ground with conventional vertical supports, braced to the seat frame. If this option is chosen

Fig 7 Bench construction

ensure that any wood in contact with the ground is tanalised.

Using lengths of 3×2in (75×50mm) PSE, manufacture four bench supports (Fig 8) to carry a seat 20–24in (500–600mm) deep and 20in (500mm) from the ground. Secure the horizontal supports to the pergola posts with two 3in (75mm) no 10 zinc screws (countersunk), and brace these supports with timber (as shown in Figs 7 and 8) so that the load is transferred through the seat to the base of the pergola posts. Provide further support with a horizontal framework bridging between supporting posts and along the front of the bench and install further cross-braces on the wide section of seating (Fig 8). If the seat is to be white-painted then the framework should now be stained to match the pergola (Fig 7).

Now secure lengths of 1½×1½in (38×38mm) PSE to the seat supports, using 2½in (63mm) no 10 zinc screws, as shown in Fig 8. Cut ends to provide neat angles and be sure to sand down any rough edges and to countersink screws.

Finally secure lengths of 3×2in (75×50mm) to provide a continuous back-rest at a convenient height. Painting should be primer, two coats of undercoat and one of gloss; or you may choose to use a white opaque wood treatment (see GCP p.56).

Trellis: On the pergola illustrated, trellis is installed on the three bench spans (Fig 9). For guidance on trellis manufacture turn to the project on trelliswork, p.68.

Fig 8 Bench construction

Fig 9 The pergola nearing completion

13 Corner house

Many properties are bounded by high walls which somewhere may provide a sunny, sheltered corner ideal for a summerhouse. Particularly in a small garden where space is at a premium, a corner house can often use space far more effectively than a free-standing structure, and provided with insulation and heat, it could very easily double as an office or play-room. This project explains the significant construction techniques required to build a three-sided timber and tile structure of unspecified dimension.

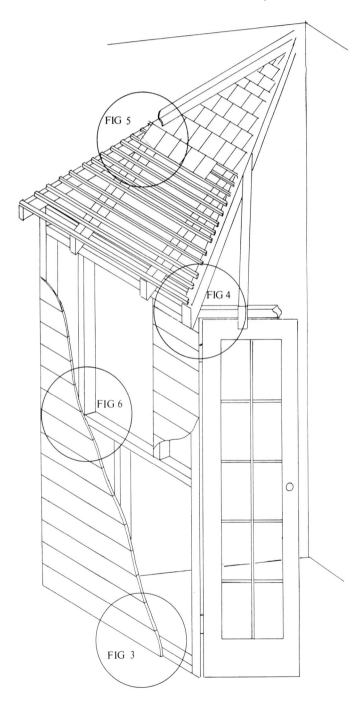

It is assumed that the reader is already conversant with the simpler construction methods; if this is not the case then you should refer to Chapter 3 General Construction Principles p.47, or to the revolving summerhouse project p.125 for background information. This applies in particular to the establishment of wall frame angles, mortice and tenon joints (refer to Footbridge project p.72) and to treatment with preservative stains p.55.

The suggested design and construction techniques that follow should give you sufficient information to adapt the structure to suit particular needs, or to come up with a different design altogether. None of the techniques is sacrosanct, but rather they are put forward as practical options, which the knowledgeable may wish to adapt. The basic design principle is that of cladding and tiling a timber carcass, fixed into a concrete base, and secured to walls (with structural integrity) using Rawl-bolts. It is assumed that planning and building regulations will not be required, although strictly this may depend on the intended use. It is particularly important to work out the *apex height* of the finished summerhouse, as it may be necessary to step up the corner wall to accommodate the structure before you even start.

Although no dimensions are specified for the overall structure the sections (thicknesses) of timber listed below will be appropriate for structures where the span of an external panel is between 4ft (1.2m) and 6ft (1.8m), giving a radius from the corner of between 7ft 7in (2.28m) and 11ft 5in (3.42m). For larger structures you should seek advice on sections of timber for roof joists and generally upgrade all supporting timbers.

MATERIALS

Base: Sub-floor of concrete (8 parts ballast to 1 part ordinary cement) on compacted surface of hardcore or stone
Heavy duty plastic membrane (damp-proof course)
Top floor of 4 parts sharp sand to 1 part ordinary cement
Wall frames: 4×2in (100×50mm) tanalised sawn softwood
Roof frames: 6×2in (150×50mm) stress-graded tanalised softwood
Wall cladding: ¾×5in (19×125mm) shiplap, or tongue and groove pine softwood
Roof cladding: ¾×1½in (19×38mm) tanalised battens
Slater's felt
Plain tiles, slates or other low-profile covering
4lb (1.8kg) lead, or adhesive bitumen/lead or bitumen/aluminium flashing
Doors/windows: Ideally French doors and matching windows in 'Georgian' style
Fixings: Galvanised nails or screws throughout. Heavy duty Rawl bolts for fixing roof and wall timbers to walls.

SPECIAL TOOLS

Circular saw with angle adjustment
Hammer drill with large masonry bit for installing Rawl bolts
Angle grinder for laying-in lead flashing and trimming slates or tiles

---

Construction

Base Before starting construction you must first establish the span of the door frame. This will usually depend on the size of doors available to you, and (in a structure with three equal faces) will decide the overall size of the structure. If this dimension is 4ft (1.2m) then the radius from the corner will be 7ft 7in (2.28m) approx; wider doors or door frame will give a longer radius.

The angle of the corner will vary – no two garden walls ever meet at the same angle – but for this project I shall assume it is 90° (the principle for assessment will be the same whatever the corner angle). There are two ways to assess your post positions: on paper, using the Sine rule formula; and on site, using pieces of string. The Sine rule is applied thus: divide the 90° corner into three 30° segments; with reference to Fig 1, BC = the span of your doors (4ft), but you need to know the radius (AB, AC) to know where to position B and C (posts). Each segment is an isosceles triangle, ie angles ABC, ACB etc are each 75° – using the Sine rule:

$$\frac{a}{\sin A} = \frac{b}{\sin B} = \frac{c}{\sin C}$$

substituting the known values of the segments:

$$\frac{a}{\sin A} = \frac{c}{\sin C}$$

$$\frac{4}{\sin 30°} = \frac{c}{\sin 75°}$$

$$\frac{4 \times \sin 75°}{\sin 30°} = c$$

Therefore c (radius) = 7.73ft (7ft 8in approx)

To establish your post positions on site: with reference to Fig 1, and armed with three 6in (150mm) nails and two bits of string at least 10ft (3m) long – divide the 90° corner into three 30° segments; place one nail, with string attached, right in the corner (the 'centre point' of a circle), and extend the sides of each segment (string) until the distance between the ends of the string is equal to the span of your chosen door span. Mark and fix this point (with the other nails) on each bit of string: these denote two post positions. With your string as radius, draw an arc – where it meets each wall defines two further post positions. This is illustrated in Fig 1.

Once the limits of the site are known and post positions established prepare the site as follows:

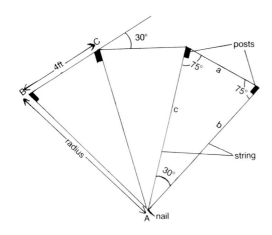

Fig 1 Post positions

Remove loose top soil and prepare a firm bed of hardcore or stone. The surface of this bed should be at least 6in (150mm) below intended floor level. Excavate rather deeper holes to receive door-frame posts, which should be set in at least 9in (228mm) of concrete (Fig 3). Place old buckets, or similar, into these two post holes, to prevent them being filled with concrete at this stage. Once the site is prepared, and the floor limits are clearly defined (ideally with wooden shuttering) begin mixing and pouring concrete, to a depth of 4in (100mm). A mix of 8 parts ballast to 1 part ordinary cement is sufficient. Indicate the level you are aiming for with marks on both walls and with wood pegs driven in to the correct level in convenient positions. Tamp the concrete down to these levels with a long piece of heavy timber, working from the corner out, and check the level with a spirit-level placed on a

substantial batten placed across adjacent pegs. Aim to achieve a reasonably level surface and allow to dry overnight protected against frost or over-rapid drying with a plastic sheet.

Damp-proof membrane: Cover the base with a heavy-duty plastic membrane lapped at least 4in (100mm) up the walls (Fig 2). If the membrane is not one piece then lap joints at least 6in (150mm). Lift out the buckets and line each of the door-frame holes to provide a continuous membrane under each post. Replace buckets and begin laying a finished floor of 4 parts sharp sand to 1 part ordinary cement. Start in the corner and level and smooth the floor as you go, finishing off with a steel trowel. The floor should be 2in (50mm) thick. Protect the finished surface from frost or over-rapid drying (which will lead to a 'sandy' finish). When dry (48 hours), trim excess plastic from the walls (leave about 6in (150mm) of plastic overhanging the front edges). You should now have an accurate, level, dry floor with two lined post sites (don't forget to remove the buckets before they set in too well).

Wall frames: With reference to Fig 2 and Fig 4 prepare wall-frame components from lengths of 4×2in (100× 50mm) tanalised timber (see Timber Treatments (GCP p.55) for guidance on the use and preparation of this timber). Before you start construction you will need to know the following, which should all be worked out and drawn up on paper with reference to the illustrations.
- Height of wall, to bottom of roof joists.
- Configuration of joints with spanning timbers (Fig 4).
- Angles required to achieve flush cladding (Multi-facet Structures GCP p.47).
- Method of fixing to walls.

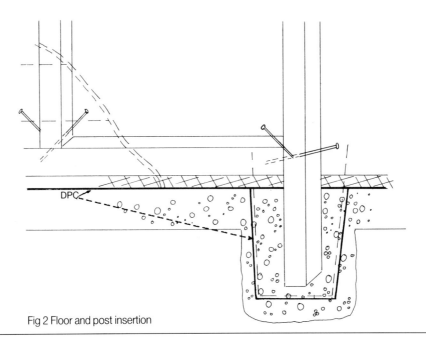

Fig 2 Floor and post insertion

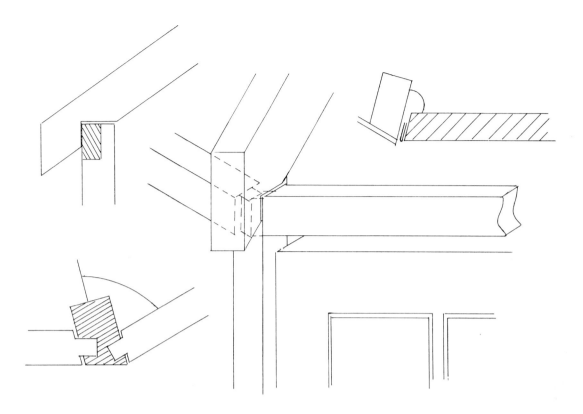

Fig 3 Details of upper frame construction

Once these points are known and understood take a length of timber nominally 78–84in (1.95–2.10m) long, and prepare it for securing (vertically) to one wall: make joints for spanning timbers at roof, window and floor levels; remove a 15° wedge from the length of one narrow side (the side to face outwards) so that it will accept the cladding spanning to the next (in this project, a door-frame) – see Chapter 3, GCP Multi-facet Structures p.48. Secure this timber to the wall with large diameter (⅜in, 10mm) Rawl-bolts. If the wall is damp you may choose to place a membrane of slater's felt between it and the timber. (Rawl-bolts work on the principle of positioning a threaded expansion sleeve into the wall and inserting into this (through object timber) a bolt which, when tightened, expands the sleeve against the sides of its hole.)

Measure and joint one door post (removing a 15° wedge of timber as before), and three spanning timbers at roof, window and floor levels (Fig 2, Fig 4) – in jointing the spanning timbers be aware that the joints will need to be angled to the posts. Assemble frame with door post in position and check the accuracy of construction by spanning with a piece of cladding.

When happy with construction, insert vertical studwork underneath the window bearer and either side of the proposed window aperture (Fig 2). Provide at least one stud per 3ft (1m) of cladding. Secure studwork with 4in (100mm) galvanised nails. Concrete the door post in its final position, taking care to check all levels first.

Repeat the operation for the opposite section, and span between the two with a joist-bearer. This timber may also define the top of the door frame, depending on your particular plan. Remember to insert joist-bearers to present their strong section against the downwards force of the roof.

Having established the complete wall frame in its finished position you will now be able to joint in and secure the roof joists. Figs 2 and 3 show the general design of main joists and additional short joists required to bear the tiling battens. The two outside joists should be bolted to the walls, and all joists secured to each other at the roof apex with nails or screws, or with steel braces. In order that tiling battens should lie flush, you should remove wedges of timber along the length of the main joists (see Multi-facet Structures for calculations p.47), in much the same way as with wall timbers. You may choose to avoid this by securing tiling battens with nails inserted at a slight angle, directly through the point of contact with the joist. Aim for a distance between joists of around 16in (400mm).

Joint each joist over the roof-bearers with a simple 'cut out' (Fig 4) and secure with galvanised nails driven from the top.

Roofing: Before you start adding further to the roof

structure decide what sort of tile or slate you wish to install and work out the correct batten spacing and laying technique for that product. Also decide how the roof will finish – will you add a fascia board? will you supply guttering? etc. One or more of these decisions may effect the position of the first (bottom) row of tiles and, consequently, decide the batten positions.

Once confident of your approach, lay slater's felt over the joists, starting from the bottom, and secure temporarily, being sure to overlap felt by at least 4in (100mm) on joins and around edge. Begin laying battens across joists at the required spacing – check the initial spacing with tiles/slates before carrying on too far. Secure battens with 2in (50mm) galvanised nails into each joist (once the correct batten spacing has been established you should prepare a spacer to speed up the fitting of battens). When walking on the roof, as you will need to do at some stage, be sure not to tread on unsupported batten or to puncture the felt with a heel or toe.

Flashing (preparation for lead flashing): If you intend to use lead flashing along the walls and over the ridges you will need to prepare a groove in the walls, into which the lead will be seated. The groove should be 1½ to 2in (38 to 50mm) deep and, if possible, angled slightly upwards in the wall, to prevent rainwater penetrating the wall via the lead. Fig 5 shows the position of lead flashing. An attractive alternative to lead flashing (which is expensive and difficult to use properly) is self-adhesive bitumen/lead, or bitumen/aluminium flashing. This will adhere to a clean dry surface very well and requires no preparation. If you do use an angle grinder be sure to wear goggles and it

may be wise to check that nobody has any washing out downwind of you. There is nothing like a cloud of brick dust to ruin a beautiful relationship.

Slating/tiling: With battening complete, begin laying tiles or slates from the bottom, completing each section of roof in turn. You should, by this time, have checked with the manufacturer or supplier what the correct installation method is for the particular system. Use an angle grinder, or circular saw with stone cutting wheel, to trim edges and corners to shape – this is all very skilled work, so do not hesitate to call in expert advice if in doubt. Pin down slates with galvanised nails as required. You will probably be using slates or tiles with self-hanging 'nibs', and nailing will be a non-essential option. Lay, or stick flashings as you go along so that you at least stand a chance of not having to climb over the completed roof. Lay lead flashing onto a bed of mastic (bituminous) to seal it, and help to hold it down and work it into shape with a light hammer and block of wood.

Cladding: With the roof complete start to apply cladding to wall sections, starting at the bottom. Use a circular saw, with blade set at the appropriate angle (15°) to prepare exact lengths. Paint any areas that will be hidden from view before fixing with galvanised nails inserted through pre-drilled holes. Use a non-oil-based system such as Sadolin for wood treatment and colour. Continue cladding right up between the joists, if necessary providing additional sections of timber for securing cladding to. Also run cladding above the door frame. If installing ready-made windows secure these in position with particular

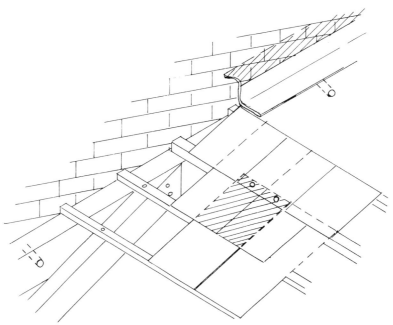

Fig 4 Detail of roof showing timber tiling and flashing

reference to the cladding, which should abut neatly against the frame.

If you intend to build your own windows a simple plan may be found in Chapter 3, GCP, p.47. Whichever windows you choose to use be sure that the window ledge 'drip' (Fig 6) is well away from the cladding. In a design sense the windows should mirror the doors: Georgian doors – Georgian windows.

Try to ensure that the bottom cladding is not in ground contact or 'bridging' the damp couirse. Tuck surplus plastic membrane down to keep the timber out of contact with the unprotected sub-floor. Trim off surplus.

Paint cladding with Sadolin or similar as you go along and with reference to manufacturer's instructions.

Having completed the roof and walls, it now only remains to fit the doors and finish off with guttering etc.

Each of the hinge sides will need to be prepared by removing a (15°) wedge of timber along its length to fit flush (unless you have made design changes). The relationship of door to door-frame is shown in Fig 3. Assess the door positions carefully before removing any timber and, once prepared, hang the doors using two or three strong brass hinges per door. When both doors are satisfacorily fitted, install door jambs in appropriate positions around and above the doors. Install door furniture as required after painting/staining.

Finishing off

Sealing joints: use a coloured mastic to seal any exposed joints, particularly against walls.

Guttering: guttering should be run to a soak-away 16ft (5m) from the structure or to a convenient water-butt.

Painting: use Sadolin Classic (PX65) or similar water-repellant treatment.

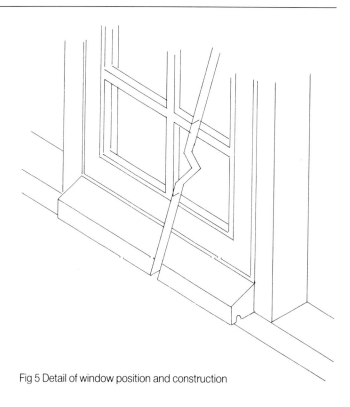

Fig 5 Detail of window position and construction

14 Simple bridge

This design is offered as an alternative to the more ornate main project, for applications where the appearance of the bridge is rather less important than its function. The design is open to interpretation and embellishment.

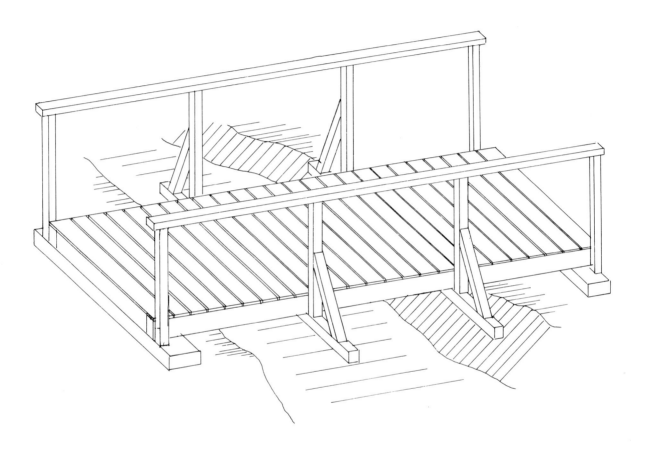

The bridge comprises a planked base laid onto substantial timber bearers; these are seated onto firm, level ground or onto a concrete foundation. The handrails are braced in a traditional way to timbers crossing underneath the bridge and extending outwards. The materials used, and the significant parts of the construction are as in the main project, see Footbridge p.72 – for long bridge spans (over 13ft (4m)) you should add additional uprights and handrail braces.

MATERIALS

Floor span: Stress-graded tanalised timbers and tanalised plank, type and dimensions as for main project

Bank bearers: Large sections of tanalised timber or railway sleepers

Uprights and braces: Lengths of 3×3in (75×75mm) tanalised timber

Handrails: Lengths of 4×2in (100×50mm) or 3×3in (75×75mm) tanalised timber

Fixings: Galvanised nails and screws plus long coach-screws for securing bearing structures to bridge timber

---

Construction

Ideally this bridge should be completely, or substantially finished before being placed in position. The following suggestions for method of construction assume that the completed framework will be swung into position and finished with the application of floor planks in-situ.

Main timbers/handrail bracing: Take two appropriate lengths of stress-graded tanalised timber (selected and prepared as for main project) and lay these *upside down* on a level surface, the chosen distance apart (width of bridge). Lay two lengths of 3×3in (75×75mm) tanalised timber across these bearers at an even spacing (⅓ and ⅔). These timbers should protrude approximately 24in (600mm) on either side of the bearers; secure them to bearers with long (6in (150mm)) coach-screws, turned into pre-drilled holes.

Turn assembly over (right way up) and measure and prepare four lengths of 3×3in (75×75mm) tanalised timber, for handrail uprights. As shown in the illustration these uprights will be jointed into the handrail with mortice and tenon joints, so before fixing in place, prepare tenons 1½in (38mm) deep and 1in (25mm) wide, using a tenon saw. Secure each post with 4in (100mm) coach-screws turned into pre-drilled holes from the *inside* face of bearers (uprights should allow for a handrail height of about 39in (1m)).

With the four uprights secured in position, brace with brackets cut at 45° and 20–24in (500–600mm) long overall – these will strengthen the handrails. Secure these braces with long zinc-plated screws, as in Fig 1.

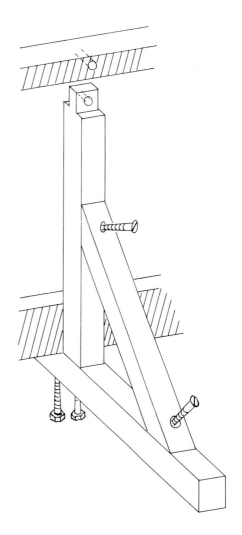

Fig 1 Simple bridge construction: detail of handrail bracing assembly

Handrails: Select and prepare (thoroughly plane and sand) two handrail lengths of 3×3in (75×75mm) or 4×2in (100×50mm) tanalised timber and lay each piece in position on uprights. Precisely mark the position and extent of the required mortices and prepare these using a 1in (25mm) flat wood bit and sharp chisel. Be careful not to allow the lead point of the wood bit to protrude through the 'wrong' side of the handrail. Advice on preparing mortices may be found in Oak Bench and Footbridge projects pp.85 and 72. You will need to provide additional uprights at each end of handrails to prevent damage to handrails.

With joints complete and tested in position, fix handrails to uprights using waterproof wood glue or cascamite. Either dowel or screw through the joints using ½in (12mm) hardwood dowel or zinc-plated screws (2½in (63mm) no 10/12). If using screws, make sure that they are countersunk so as not to present any sharp edges along the handrail.

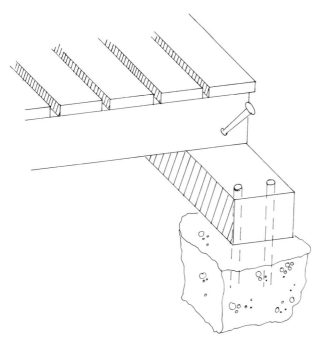

Fig 2 Bridge base bearing on timber ragbolted to concrete foundation

Positioning: Before positioning the bridge frame prepare a substantial bearing foundation, using large sections of treated timber – possibly fixed to a concrete base with ragbolts inserted through timbers into 'wet' concrete. Use a spirit-level to ensure level. Lay the bridge structure onto these bearers and fix with long galvanised nails, driven through the main bearers (Fig 2).

Plank floor: With the bridge frame in position begin laying planks for the floor ($7 \times 1\frac{1}{2}$in (175×38mm) tanalised plank) – see Footbridge p.72. Secure planks with 3in (75mm) galvanised nails or screws, allowing a space between them for removal of surface water; space evenly along the length of bridge, aiming to finish with a complete width of plank.

With the bridge complete, build up the bank on either side to provide level or gently sloping access at plank level. Providing you have used tanalised timber during construction you may pack earth around the base structure without fear of degrading the timber.

15 Garden and patio whatnot

The reader may well have come across, or own, a traditional whatnot – a light piece of furniture with a number of shelves usually used for displaying small treasured articles or bric à brac within the home. They are usually antiques of some value and are displayed and used as such. In a way it is a shame that such a potentially useful piece of design tends to be limited in its use by its own value, and this project suggests a design for a garden and patio whatnot for use as an occasional table for food and drinks, or as a plant stand. Made from treated timbers, and coloured with a preservative stain or timber treatment, this whatnot may be left out all the year round, or perhaps taken into the conservatory to continue a useful role during the winter months. The imaginative reader will realise the potential for changing the suggested design to suit a particular purpose. It may be that a simple square whatnot will fit into a corner nicely, or a round one will complement some existing patio furniture. There is also scope for the use of different materials and finishes.

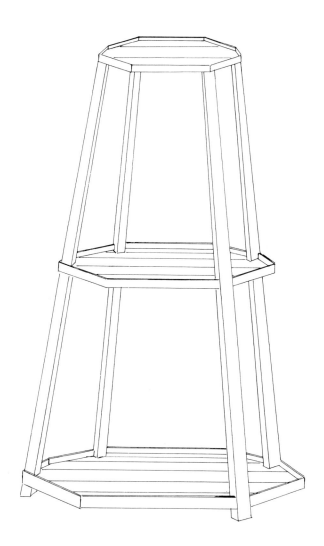

I have used tongue and groove boards because I find them both attractive and flexible in application. They can be used efficiently, with very little waste, and are extremely versatile. The pyramidal shape of the whatnot fulfils two functions. It is an attractive and practical form, allowing access to lower shelves, and also contributes greatly to the stability and rigidity of the structure. Fine pieces of furniture with delicate legs and fine balance are all very well in the house, but not so good in the garden.

MATERIALS

To make a three tier octagonal whatnot with shelf sizes 28in (700mm), 21in (525mm) and 14in (350mm) at widest point.

Timber: 33ft (10m) of 1×5in (25×125mm) tongue and groove softwood board (tanalised or vacuum treated ideally)

10ft (3m) of ¾×1½in (19×38mm) tanalised softwood batten

15ft 8in (4.8m) (divisible by 47in (1.2m)) of 2×2in (50×50mm) tanalised softwood

16ft (5m) of ½×2in (12×50mm) (approx) softwood trim

12in (300mm) of ½in (12mm) hardwood dowel

Fixings: Small head galvanised nails 1½in (38mm)

Sharadised panel pins 1in (25mm)

Zinc-plated screws 8×3in (75mm) no 10, 8×2in (50mm) no 8 or 10

Waterproof wood glue

Finish: Sadolin or similar preservative finish, Pinotex or similar microporous wood treatment

TOOLS

Ordinary DIY tools will suffice for this project although a jig saw and/ or circular saw will certainly speed things up.

Dimensions

The aim is to produce three shelves of diminishing size that will be joined together by four legs. In Fig 1 the reclining angle of each leg is 10°. The height *(from bottom edge of bottom shelf to bottom edge of top shelf)* is 39in (1m) and the width (at widest) of the bottom shelf is 28in (700mm). The starting point for this, and any other, design are these factors: 1 required height; 2 reclining angle; 3 base dimension.

Given a 10° angle and known base dimension, it will be clear to you that the dimension of the middle and top shelves at any given height is pre-determined: in this instance 21in (525mm) middle and 14in (350mm) top (see Fig 1a). The relationship between these dimensions (reducing 7in (175mm) per shelf) is mathematical and predictable for any chosen angle and bottom shelf dimension. Say, for example, that you wish to angle your whatnot at 20°, with a base dimension of 36in (900mm), then the top shelf (at 28in (700mm) height) will be 15.2in (380mm) wide, and the middle shelf 25.6in (640mm), the gradation being 10.4in (264mm) reduction per shelf. Armed with this knowledge, a piece of graph paper, a ruler

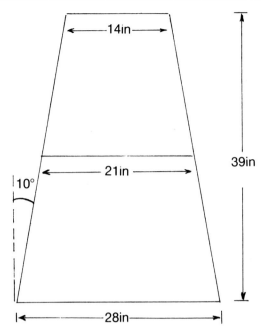

Fig 1 Shelf dimensions, angle and height

and protractor, you should be able to work out a design of size and style to suit your particular requirements.

Whatever dimensions you ultimately choose the construction will be similar and, for the purposes of this project, the original dimensions are assumed.

Construction

Shelves: Produce shelves of 28in (700mm), 21in (525mm) and 14in (350mm) diameter (point to point) using the procedure outlined for production of dovecote base (p.00) with the following additions/alterations.

1 Treat tongues and grooves of timber with chosen stain or treatment prior to assembly.

2 Do not allow supporting battens to extend within 1½in (38mm) of any outside edge (to allow room for leg insertion). This requirement will prohibit the use of very narrow sections of TG board on the 'outside' of shelves as these will be unsupported (see Fig 2).

3 Fix battens with widest dimension (1½in (38mm)) to base of shelves (rather than the narrowest, as in the dovecote project).

4 Nail (or screw) through batten into base of shelf, rather than through shelf into batten. No screws or nails should be seen on shelf surfaces.

Fig 2 shows construction of (bottom) shelf and in particular the position of battens in relation to leg joints.

Leg joints: Provision should be made for the jointing of legs into shelves. Figs 2 and 3 suggest one method of jointing, which relies on the provision of brackets to support bottom and middle shelves. It may be that you

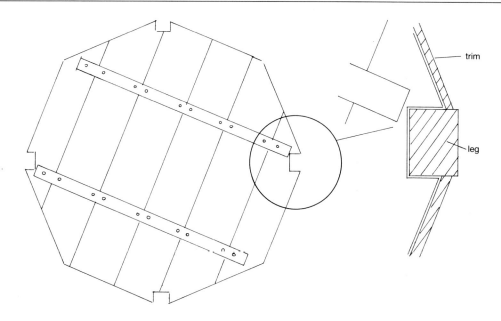

Fig 2 Construction of bottom shelf, showing joints for legs and position of legs and trim

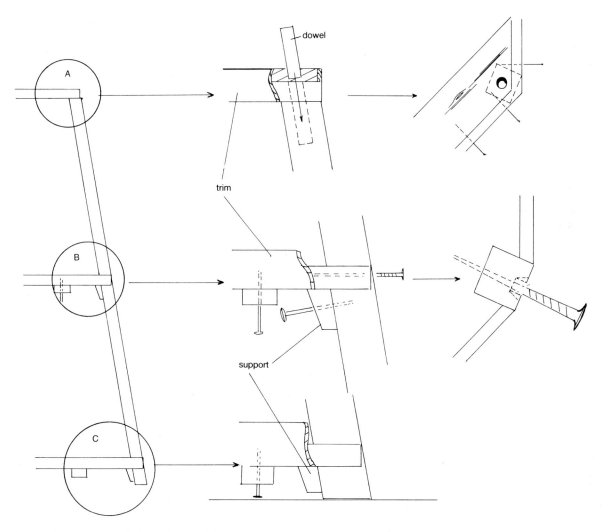

Fig 3 Sections to show assembly of whatnot legs and shelves

choose to cut a joint from the leg itself, to slot around the shelves, and this will be very satisfactory. Whatever method is chosen remember that you must compensate for the 10° inclination of the legs in preparation of joints, brackets etc. Also remember to take into account the thickness of trim to be applied later (see Figs 1, 2 and 3).

Note on size of joint and thickness of legs: 2×2in (50× 50mm) timber will actually finish at rather less than this (usually 1¾in (44mm) square). Coupled with the need for the outside face of each leg to finish proud of trim, you will be looking to cut a joint of no more than 1⅛in (28mm) in from each point. Be sure to assess the requirement accurately before cutting.

Legs: In this project the legs are shown as square (2×2in (50×50mm)) posts, set into the shelves. There is obviously scope for routing, planing or other decorative embellishment, such as reduction of thickness from bottom to top so that the small top shelf is supported by rather more slender legs.

Length of legs: In the first instance prepare 4×47in (1.2m) lengths of timber. Plane, chamfer and sand smooth as required. These lengths allow for legs below bottom shelf of up to 7½in (187.5mm).

Decide what length is required (allowing for supporting battens on bottom shelf; the minimum for ground clearance should be 41in (1025mm)).

Cut ONE leg to length by removing timber from both ends so that, when tilted at 10° both top and bottom present level faces (to top shelf and ground) (see Fig 3).

Carry out a trial fitting of this leg before preparing others.

Assembly of legs and shelves: The suggested means of assembly is as illustrated in Fig 3, using a single 3in (75mm) zinc-plated screw driven into a deeply countersunk pre-drilled hole through each leg into each shelf at each joint. This fixing should then be reinforced with a small wooden bracket (made from waste board) glued and screwed to the inside of legs at middle and bottom shelf.

Before drilling and fixing in any way the shelves and legs should be dry assembled to ensure they are fit and level. With shelves in position mark drill points on outside and shelf positions on inside of legs. Using waterproof wood glue fix bottom and middle shelves.

With bottom and middle shelves fixed in position, place top shelf on legs and assess position for dowel posts before drilling with flat wood bit down through shelf into legs. Insert dowels with waterproof wood glue and saw, or chisel, and smooth surface.

Trim: With structure complete prepare lengths of ½in (12mm) trim to fix around the edge of shelves. Set the trim to provide a lip to each shelf of up to 1in (25mm) height. Fix with wood glue and 1in (25mm) sharadised panel pins.

Stain and treatment: With the whatnot complete apply timber treatment, stain or decorative finish to manufacturers' instructions.

16 Bird table

The accompanying figure proposes the construction of a simple covered bird table, of the sort often seen in gardens. As a matter of design, it seems to me that a structure intended to sit in a prominent position and attract beautiful birds should be built and finished so that it is very attractive itself. This requires the use of good quality, planed timber and the application of attractive colour – as well as the use of reasonable techniques during construction. A few bits of branch joined together with rusty nails can never conform to this standard!

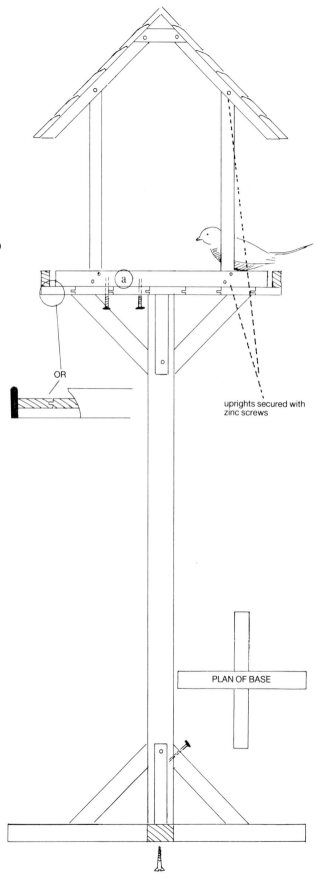

uprights secured with zinc screws

OR

PLAN OF BASE

Fig 1 The bird table, with detail of base construction

MATERIALS

Post and (ground) cross-pieces: 3×3in (75×75mm) tanalised softwood

Supporting brackets: 2×2in (50×50mm) tanalised softwood

Table: 1×5in (25×125mm) tongue and groove floorboard

Table frame/raised lip: 1×1½in (25×38mm) PSE (planed square edge) batten

Roof supports: 1½×1½in (38×38mm) PSE softwood

Roof: ¾×5in (19×125mm) shiplap

Roof frame: 1×1½in (25×38mm) PSE batten

Apex trim: Birdsmouth hardwood moulding (or similar)

Fixings: Zinc-plated screws, galvanised nails

Treatment/colour: Sadolin Pinotex Superdec, Sadolin Classic or similar treatments

Construction

In general the construction of this item should be obvious from Fig 1 and from your own experience of this type of simple project. The following notes cover the more critical points of construction and design.

Stand: Stand cross-timbers should be of 3×3in (75×75mm) tanalised timber – with two lengths, slightly wider than the bird table (for stability), joined together at their centres with a half-lap joint. The main post, of 3×3in (75×75mm) tanalised timber, should be screwed to this cross base and bracketed with lengths of 2×2in (50×50mm) tanalised softwood, cut to form 45° brackets, and secured with zinc-plated screws or galvanised nails, inserted through pre-drilled holes. Four more brackets should be prepared for securing table to post.

Table: To hold small bird seeds and other bird foods the table top should be solid and bordered with a raised edge (to prevent feed spilling, or being blown onto the ground). An assembly of tongue and groove floor-boards should be glued and screwed to lengths of planed softwood batten (1½×2in (38×50mm)) to form the required rectangular or square shape (see Fig 1). The batten will serve as the raised edge of the table and screws should be inserted through the boards into the battens so that the screw-heads will be underneath the table in final position (see **a** in Fig 1). Leave a small gap in each corner to allow drainage of surface water.

Roof: Create a framework of 1×1½in (25×38mm) batten and clad with shiplap timber, finishing at the apex with a length of hardwood moulding covering the joint. The frame should be built so that it may be joined to the table frame by lengths of 1½×1½in (38×38mm) PSE softwood running from the 'inside' of the roof frame batten to the 'inside' of the table frame batten using zinc-plated screws (see Fig 1). Brace roof structure with cross-pieces of batten near the apex and aim to allow the roof to slightly overlap the table so that most of the rainwater will fall directly to the ground.

Finish the structure with the application of wood treatment and colour, using water or spirit-based systems such as Sadolin Pinotex or Sadolin Classic. Do not use oil-based systems unless you are prepared for the bother of re-painting.

To prevent wind damage, the structure should be secured in position with lengths of heavy steel wire pushed into the ground and bent over each of the supporting cross-pieces.

If the bird table is to be placed in a permanent position you may consider putting the post into a concrete foundation or metal sleeve.

Index

Arboured path (Project 1), 64–7

Bench
    Covered, 12
    Curved, 18
    Oak (Project 5), 85–91
    Stone, 18
Bird houses, 16, 41 *see also* Dovecote
Birdtable (Project 16), 157–8
Bridges
    Arched, 12
    Footbridge (Project 3), 72–7
    Timber and steel, 26
    Simple bridge (Project 14), 150–2

Carving, 91
Chair (garden), 43
Circular saw
    Description, 57
    Techniques, 49, 50, 57
Colour, 9
Corner house (Project 13), 144–9
Covered seat, 12

Deck, 35
Dovecotes, 16
Dovecote projects (8 and 9)
    Cottage dovecote, 102–16
    Wall-mounted, 117–20
Doves, 116
Dowelling, 75; techniques for tight
    jointing, 54

Electrical supply
    Armoured cable, 128, 129
    Fused fittings, 135
English garden, 10–25

Fences, 28, 29
Fixings (nails, screws etc), 57
Flashing, 148
Formal perspective, 25

Frames
    Preparation of wall/roof frames for
    multi-facet projects, 50ff, 104, 109

Gate (Project 10), 121–4
Gazebo, 43
General construction principles, 47–62
Glazing, 53

Jig one, wall section assembly, 50, 51
Jig two, roof sections, 52
Jig saw, 58

Lakeside pavilion, 41

Martin house, 41
Mathematics, 47, 48, 145
Mortices
    Techniques for tight jointing, 54

New England garden, 26–46

Oak bench (Project 5), 85–91
Oak, buying, 86

Pergola (Project 12), 136–42
Pergola (rustic), 39
Picnic table (Project 6), 92–5
Plane, 58
Plywood inserts, 114
Polesden Lacey, 10
Porch, 21, 30
Position and proportion, 6, 7

Rawlbolts, 118
Revolving summerhouse (Project 11),
    125–35
Roof angles, 47
Roof cladding, 111
Roof sections, sectional construction, 47
Roofing (tiles), 148
Router, 58
Rustic pergola, 39
Rustic swinging chair, 44

Sadolin Pinotex Superdec, 14
Safety, 84
Satellite dishes, 44
Seats
    Covered, 12
    Curved, 18
    Stone, 18
    Swinging, 36
Sheds, 36
Shingles, 31, 34
Simple bridge (Project 14), 150–2
Soakaway, 149
Steelwork, 125–35
Summerhouses, 21, 31, 34
Summerhouse (Project 11), 125–35

Template construction
    Walls, wall cladding, 48
    Wall and roof frames, 50
Tenons, techniques for tight jointing, 54
Timber, 54
    Buying, 57
    Grading, 56
    Sizes, 56
    Tanalising, 55
    Treatments, 55
Tools, 57
Tree house (Project 7), 96, 101
Trellis (Project 2), 68–71
Trellised porch, 21, 30

Wall sections
    Jig assembly, 50
    Sectional construction, 47
Water, using power tools near, 84
Weathervane, 11
Whatnot (Project 15), 153–6
Wildfowl nesting box (Project 4), 78–84
Windows, simple construction, 53
Wisteria, 68
Wood *see* timber
Wood treatment, 14
Wrought iron gazebo, 43

ACKNOWLEDGEMENTS

The author would like to thank the following people who contributed in one way or another to the completion of this book: Julian and Diane Thompson, for services to my psyche; Margaret Kirk (née Smith), for the mathematics; Margaret Smith, my mother-in-law, for helping me out of a corner; Sean Leahy, for his work in the darkroom; Jack Hill, for his constructive criticism during editing; all at David & Charles, and Sue Hall in particular, for giving me such an easy time of it.